'In a nation as humourless
as us Indians, joke books sell
like hot pakoras...'

Khushwant

## Khushwant Singh
### in the words of his son Rahul Singh

'In his long and distinguished career, (Khushwant Singh) tried his hand at almost anything that came his way. He has, in turn, been a lawyer, a diplomat, a broadcaster (he has a very good voice) a United Nations official, an academic, a historian, an editor, a syndicated columnist, an author and a publishing consultant. In between, he has often been jobless. And now he does what he enjoys the most: writing, provoking and making people laugh.'

In a nation of singularly humourless people, his ability to make us laugh at our own foibles has earned him the sobriquet of 'the greatest humourist of modern India' and the accolade of 'master spinner of jokes'.

This master craftsman of his art was born in Lahore (1915) and now lives in Delhi devoting his time to writing and other literary activities.

# Khushwant Singh's

Joke 9 Book

Orient
Paperbacks
DELHI | MUMBAI | HYDERABAD

ISBN: 978-81-222-0513-8

*Khushwant Singh's Joke Book 9*

Subject: Humour / Jokes

© Mala Dayal

1st Published 2012

Published by
**Orient Paperbacks**
(A division of Vision Books Pvt. Ltd.)
5A/8, Ansari Road, New Delhi-110 002)
www.orientpapberbacks.com

Cover Illustration Courtesy: Ajit Ninan / India Today
Inside Illustrations by Uday Shankar

Printed at
Anand Sons, Delhi-110 092, India

Cover Printed at
Ravindra Printing Press, Delhi-110 006, India

## PREFACE

I was 94 when Joke Book 8 was published. I was sure that it would be the last of the joke books that I would compile. I was on a diet of pills and in poor health. But here I am 97 years old and here is Joke Book 9 — laughter is evidently the elixir of life. The best tonic in the world to ensure a long and happy life.

Laughter is not only the best tonic but humorous writing and relating other people's jokes is very lucrative as both my publishers and I have found. Everyone of the earlier books in the series has gone into more than a dozen reprints. They are to be seen on pavement, railway station and airport bookstalls.

But not everyone enjoys jokes, especially when they are the target. This is especially true of politicians who have notoriously thin skins. We have has quite a few very good cartoonists — Shankar Pillai, R K Laxman, Vijayan, Rajinder Puri, Mario Miranda. Their cartoons have enlivened our newspapers and magazines and brought a smile on our faces. But many politicians and political parties take themselves very seriously and consider far too many topics as sacred cows not to be laughed about. They take umbrage at being the butt of jokes.

Laughter for them is no laughing matter. They serve who poke fun at them with legal notices — or worse.

I cannot take credit for the jokes appearing in the book. A large number were sent to me by readers who have been acknowledged by their names. Some I made up or moulded from jokes I picked up from friends, books and magazines.

At the end of the day, more than my other work as a novelist, short story writer, historian of the Sikhs or translator, I am known for my joke books. At every gathering, I am implored, *'Koi joke-shoke ho jai'* — let there be a joke or two. I am known as a joker.

September, 2012
New Delhi

## FOGGED OUT

**S**anta while out driving one morning, lost his way, since the visibility was down to nearly zero due to heavy fog. To be safe, he decided to closely follow a car that was driving in front of him and, when it slowed down, overtake and ask the driver where they were.

The car in front, after driving for some time, suddenly without any warning stopped, causing Santa's car to bump into it. The driver of the car got out and started shouting at Santa.

'It's not my fault,' Santa shouted back. 'How can you stop so suddenly, without giving any indication or warning?' The driver of the other car looked at Santa queerly, and asked in surprise. 'You want me to give an indication that I am going to stop inside my own garage?'

*Contributed by Rajeshwari Singh, Delhi*

## SAD DAY

**W**hat is the Day of Judgment?

When Valentine's Day and Raksha Bandhan fall on the same day.

*Contributed by J P Singh Kaka, Bhopal*

## TWO-PIECE COVERING

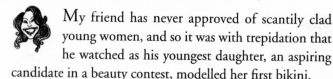

My friend has never approved of scantily clad young women, and so it was with trepidation that he watched as his youngest daughter, an aspiring candidate in a beauty contest, modelled her first bikini.

'Look, Daddy,' she said, 'I bought this with the birthday money you and mom gave me.'

My friend stared, glared and then snapped, 'We didn't give you much, did we?'

*Contributed by Reeten Ganguly, Tezpur*

## FALSE TEST

Several young boys were rounded up by Delhi police for a medical check-up to determine the paternity of a certain teenage girl's baby.

Chandulal went in and after a few minutes came out: 'Don't worry, fellows,' he smiled. 'They'll never find out. They're taking samples from the finger.'

*Contributed by Anirban Sen, New Delhi*

## NO ROOM FOR BAPU

**A** managing director of a company was distressed to find that many men working under him had been found guilty of corruption. In order to teach others a lesson, he proposed to the Board of Directors that they put pictures of the corrupt men on the walls of the main reception room just as the police display photographs of criminals in the main hall of the police station.

Hearing this, the youngest member of the Board remarked: 'If we do so, there will be no room left for photographs of Mahatma Gandhi and Prime Minister Manmohan Singh.'

*Contributed by Ramesh Kotian Udupi, S. Kanara*

## PURE TRUTH

**M**essage from Sri Ravishankar in Goa:

Having a wife is part of living. But having a girl friend along with a wife is 'Art of Living'.

*Contributed by Vipin Buckshey, New Delhi*

## CARRYING YOUR BURDEN

 **A** husband comes home from *satsang* and greets his wife, lifts her up and carries her around the house.

His wife is surprised and asks, 'Did the Swamiji preach about being romantic today?'

Her husband replies, 'No, he said we must carry our burdens and sorrows with a smile.'

*Contributed by Vipin Buckshey, New Delhi*


## BOSOM POWER

 **A** would-be actress used to boast that her motto was 'Bollywood or Bust'.

One of her friends asked her what it meant.

She replied, 'It means that if I can't get a break into Hindi films as I am, I will go and get implants done to improve my figure.'

*Contributed by Rajeshwari Singh, New Delhi*

**R**am: 'My father owned the whole of Ayodhya and they are giving me 500 square metres and expect me to be satisfied.'

Sita: 'If that is all we are getting, and with food prices hitting the roof, how will we survive. I think I'll open a travel agency to earn some money.'

Laxman: 'I've spent years facing high speed missiles, thrown by foreign demons, in order to defend the country. I think I can face them for a few more years.'

Shatrughan: 'Royalty is defunct, so I am going to become a politician. I hear that it is a lucrative profession.'

Ravan: 'I seem to have become unpopular. People just don't come to see my latest public appearance.'

*Contributed by Rajeshwari Singh, New Delhi*

## IN PRAISE OF TAJ

**W**hen we see the Taj Mahal at Agra we say, *'Wah* Taj!' But when we see the Taj Hotel in Mumbai we say, *'Ah,* Taj'.

*Contributed by K J S Ahluwalia, Amritsar*

The following parody of Robert Frost's 'Stopping By Woods on a Snowy Evening' makes good reading.

Whose jobs are these, don't want to know
    Paid heavily each month without fail though;
Boss hasn't time for looking here,
    To see on the files the dust grow.

My ballpoint pen may think it queer,
    To start without an envelope near;
Between the nods and a handshake
    The file progresses in minutes mere.

Boss gives his head a vigorous shake
    To ask if there is any mistake;
Some part of my earnings he does reap,
    We all have and eat our cake.

The chair is cosy and files in heap
    But I have a family to keep;
And hours to sleep before the nation's leap
    And hours to sleep before the nation's leap.

*Contributed by Sikand Shukla, Allahabad*

## LOVE MAKES MAD

 **A** lady who was not keeping too well asked her husband, 'How much do you love me?'

Man: 'So much that after your death I will go mad.'

Wife: 'Will you remarry?'

Man: 'What can one say! A mad man can do anything.'

*Contributed by Kuldip Salil, Delhi*


## REPARTEE

 **M**ani Shankar Aiyar has probably not read Dale Carnegie's bestseller, *How to Win Friends and Influence People.*

A few years ago, in the St Stephen's College alumni register, former External Affairs Minister Natwar Singh wrote, 'I am what I am because of the college.'

Prompt came Aiyar's rejoinder, 'Why blame the college!'

*Rajdeep Sardesai in Hindustan Times*

## THE ROYAL FART

 '**B**reaking news' from London, during President Obama's visit:

President and the Queen are proceeding towards Buckingham Palace in the Queen's carriage, waving to thousands of cheering Britons; all is going well. Suddenly the right rear horse lets fly the most horrendous earth shattering fart ever heard in the British Empire. The smell is atrocious and both passengers in the carriage must use handkerchiefs to cover their noses.

The Queen turns to her guest, 'Mr President, please accept my regrets... I'm sure you understand there are some things that even a Queen cannot control!'

In his best Presidential style replied Obama: 'Your Majesty, please don't give the matter another thought... Until you mentioned it, I thought it was one of the horses.'

*Contributed by Paramjit S Kochar, Delhi*

## ONE MAN PARTY

**W**ho constitutes 'A' to 'Z' of Pakistan's People Party?
Asif Zardari.

*Contributed by K J S Ahluwalia, Amritsar*

In the days when you couldn't count on a public toilet facility, an English-woman was planning a trip to India. She was registered to stay in a guesthouse owned by the local schoolmaster. She was concerned as to whether the guesthouse contained a WC. In England, a bathroom is commonly called a WC — or Water Closet. She wrote to the schoolmaster inquiring of the facilities about the WC.

The schoolmaster asked the local priest if he knew the meaning of WC. Together, they pondered possible meanings of the letters and concluded that the lady wanted to know if there was a 'Wayside Chapel' near the house... A bathroom never entered their minds.

So the schoolmaster replied:

'I take pleasure in informing you that a WC is located nine miles from the house. It is located in the middle of a grove of pine trees, surrounded by lovely grounds. It is capable of holding 229 people and is open on Sundays and Thursdays. As there are many people expected in the summer months, I suggest you arrive early. There is, however, plenty of standing room. This is an unfortunate situation especially if you are in the habit of going regularly. It may be of some interest to you that my daughter was married in the WC as it was there that she met her husband. It was a wonderful event. There were 10 people in every seat. It was wonderful to see the expressions on their faces. We can take photos in different angles. My wife, sadly, has been ill and unable to go recently. It has been almost a year since she went last, which pains her greatly.

'You will be pleased to know that many people bring their lunch and make a day of it... I would recommend your ladyship to plan to go on a Thursday, as there is an organ accompaniment. The acoustics are excellent and even the most delicate sounds can be heard everywhere... We are holding a bazaar to provide plush seats for all since many feel it is long needed. I look forward to escorting you there myself and seating you in a place where you can be seen by all.'

The woman fainted reading the reply — and she never visited India!!!

*Contributed by Vipin Buckshey, New Delhi*

## CRIME AND PUNISHMENT

Pakistani to American: 'What do you guys do with thieves?'

American: 'We treat them humanely and give them nice food, warm clothes and long jury trials.'

Pakistani: 'That's nothing. We give them the Presidency.'

*Contributed by Faisal Aziz, Karachi*

# FILE IT, FORGET IT

This is a true story of an ingenious politician who was head of a government company which was to buy 40 new buses for its transport fleet.

After getting his palm duly greased, he asked his procurement-in-charge to put up a note recommending that the buses be bought from a particular firm. The note was duly put up. The politician wrote 'Approved' below the note and signed.

Meanwhile, another firm had got wind of the deal, so they approached the politician with a better kick-back offer. The politician recalled the file and added 'Not' in front of 'Approved'.

The original supplier then landed up and offered the politician a further cut. The politician calmly recalled the file a second time and added an 'e' after 'Not', so that now it read 'Note Approved'.

*Contributed by Rajeshwari Singh, New Delhi*

# POWER FAILURE

The electric train at the suburban station was delayed because of a power failure. When irate commuters complained, the station master retorted: 'I am powerless in this matter.'

*Contributed by Paramjit S Kochar, New Delhi*

# GIVE IT A THOUGHT

 One day Emperor Akbar asked Birbal what he would choose if he were given a choice between justice and a gold coin?

'The gold coin,' said Birbal without hesitation.

The Emperor was taken aback. 'You would prefer a gold coin to justice?' he asked incredulously. 'Yes,' said Birbal.

The other courtiers were amazed by Birbal's display of idiocy. For years, they had been trying to discredit Birbal in the Emperor's eyes but without success and now the man had gone and done it himself! They could not believe their good fortune.

'I would have been dismayed if even the lowliest of my servants had said this,' continued the Emperor. 'But coming from you... it's shocking and sad. I did not know you were so debased.'

Replied Birbal politely, 'One asks for what one does not have, Your Majesty! You have seen to it that in our country justice is available to everybody. And because justice is already available but I am always short of money, I opted for the gold coin.'

The Emperor was so pleased with Birbal's reply that he gave him not one but a thousand gold coins!

*Contributed by Vipin Buckshey, New Delhi*

## MICHELLE'S HUSBAND

**O**ne night President Obama and his wife Michelle decided to do something out of routine and go for a casual dinner at a restaurant that wasn't too luxurious. When they were seated, the owner of the restaurant asked the president's secret service if he could please speak to the First Lady in private.

They obliged, and Michelle had a conversation with the owner.

Following this conversation President Obama asked Michelle, why was the owner so interested in talking to her. She replied that in her teenage years, he had been madly in love with her.

Hearing this President Obama quipped, 'So if you had married him, you would now be the owner of this lovely restaurant.'

Responded Michelle, 'No, if I had married him, he would now have been the President.'

*Contributed by Vipin Buckshey, New Delhi*

## HAPPY EVER AFTER

**E**very wife is a miss for an hour and stress for 23 hours.

*Contributed by Paramjit S Kochar, Delhi*

## MANTRIJI'S STOMACH

**A** doctor was called for as *mantriji* was suffering from upset stomach and had been to the toilet thrice. The doctor asked his wife, 'What did he eat last night?' His wife said, 'Rs 5 crore or more for a land deal, I guess.'

'I mean, what did he have for dinner?' clarified the doctor, even as the minister's PA blushed and the minister let out an uncomfortable groan. The wife said, 'Oh, he ate only two *chapattis* with *saag-paneer*. Before that he had taken a drink of scotch and soda.' The doctor pronounced, 'Either the water or the *paneer* could be the reason behind the upset stomach.'

While the doctor went ahead with checking *mantriji's* BP, the PA phoned some officials of the water filter company and ordered them to come and immediately examine the machine. The wife vouched for the freshness of *saag* but wasn't much sure about the *paneer*. The PA then instructed the food department to raid the shop from where the *paneer* was brought.

At that point the servant cut in, 'But Dr Sahib, *mantriji* dashed to the toilet as soon as he opened the newspaper this morning.' Puzzled the doctor asked for the newspaper which was promptly produced. He looked at the headline and said, 'Yes, that seems to be the root cause. It says WikiLeaks will upload the list of those persons who have hidden money in Swiss banks.'

*Contributed by Jaspal Bhatti, Chandigarh*

## FALSETTO

**S**anta was very proud of his voice and loved singing. One Diwali night he invited his friends for drinks, and to hear him sing.

When everyone was in the mood, he stood up to sing the latest hit from Bollywood. As he struck a high note, his upper denture fell out. He put it back in his mouth. When he struck a low note, his lower denture fell out. He put it back. While he was thinking how to strike the right note, one of his friends shouted: 'O Santaya, will you sing something or just keep changing cassettes?'

*Contributed by Harjeet Charanjit Singh, New Delhi*

## GHOST DRIVER

**S**anta was taking an evening walk, when it started to rain. To his relief, a car coming slowly towards him stopped next to where he was standing. Santa opened its door and jumped in. Once inside, he realised that there was no one else in the car. Thinking the car to be haunted, Santa started screaming.

Then he heard Banta's voice, *'Oye* Santa, what are you shouting for? Instead of sitting inside, come out and help me to push the car. I have run out of petrol.'

*Contributed by Rajeshwari Singh, New Delhi*

**A** group of young women decided to arrange for a camp with their mothers-in-law to hopefully get to know and understand one another better since relations between them were very sour.

Two buses were hired, one for the mothers-in-law and the other for the daughters-in-law. Unfortunately, the bus in which the mothers-in-law were travelling was involved in an accident and all passengers died on the spot.

The daughters-in-law (women being women) shed a few tears but they were all puzzled by one woman who wailed uncontrollably for what they perceived to be her great personal loss.

One woman asked her, 'Forgive me for asking, but why are you crying so hard? I didn't realise you were so close to your mother-in-law?'

'No we are not close at all, she missed the bus!' she replied.

*Contributed by Vipin Buckshey, Delhi*

## ART NOUVEAU

There is an art to release a fart,
   At the National Gallery of Modern Art!

*Contributed by A K Mittal, Delhi*

# ONE-LINERS

Everyone is ignorant, only on different subjects.

☺

The best way to succeed in life is to act on the advice you give to others.

☺

You will never be on top of the world if you try to carry it on your shoulders.

☺

If at first you don't succeed, you're running about average.

*Contributed by Shall, Minnesota, U.S.A.*

## CHALLANED!

 **S**anta was caught for speeding and was produced before the magistrate.

Magistrate: 'What'll you take? 30 days or Rs 3000?'

Santa: 'I think I'll take the money.'

*Contributed by Vijay Sharma, Dharmashala*

## RELIGIOUS EDUCATION

 A Catholic priest, a Hindu guru, and a Taliban mullah all served as religious advisers to the theological students at Harvard University. They would get together every week over tea for discussions.

They agreed that preaching to men and women was not very difficult. The real challenge would be to preach to animals. They decided to conduct an experiment. They would go to the jungle, find a bear, preach to it, and attempt to convert it.

A month later they all met to discuss their experiences. The priest, who had his arm in a sling and bandages all over his body, spoke first, 'I went to an African jungle and when I found a bear I read to him from the Holy Book. But the bear began to slap me around. So I grabbed my holy water, sprinkled him and, holy Mary Mother of Christ, he became as gentle as a lamb. The Pope is coming next week to give him first communion and confirmation.'

The guru spoke next. He was in a wheelchair with an IV drip and both legs in casts. In his best fiery oratory he exclaimed: 'Brothers, I went to Indian jungles. I found a bear and read to it from our Hindu holy book. But the bear wanted nothing to do with me. So we began to wrestle. We wrestled down one hill, up another until we came to the Ganges River. I dunked him and his hairy soul in the water. And just like you said, he became gentle as a lamb. We spent the rest of the day praising Lord Shiva.'

The priest and the guru now looked towards the mullah, who was lying in a bed. He was in a body cast with monitors and IV's running in and out of him. He looked up and said, 'Looking back, I don't think it was a good idea to start by first circumcising the bear...'

*Contributed by Vipin Buckshey, New Delhi*

## DEAR BROTHER-IN-LAW

**A** man suffered a serious heart attack and had an open-heart bypass surgery. He awakened from the surgery to find himself in the care of nuns at a Catholic hospital. As he was recovering, a nun asked him how he would like to pay for his treatment and if he had health insurance.

In a raspy voice he replied, 'No health insurance'. The nun further asked if he had money in the bank? He replied, 'No money in the bank.'

'Do you have a relative who could help you?' She questioned. He said, 'I only have a spinster sister, who is a nun.' The nun became agitated and announced loudly, 'Nuns are not spinsters: Nuns are married to God.'

'In that case,' the patient replied, 'send the bill to my brother-in-law.'

*Contributed by J P Singh Kaka, Bhopal*

## PM: My Cabinet is more cohesive than Nehru's

Mani Shankar Aiyar says no, it isn't; Chidambaram says yes, it is.

A. Raja says let's hope it never is; Kamal Nath says of course it is.

Digvijay Singh says don't be silly; Montek says Kamal Nath is wrong and Mamata says rifts are the work of the CPI(M).

## Pak High Commissioner on Match-fixing

Pak match-fixing scandal is an Indian conspiracy and other Indian plots include the bomb blasts in Pakistan, the Taliban, Osama bin Laden and the floods.

## PM: Not possible to distribute free food to 37 per cent of population below the poverty line

'A Right to Malnutrition Act should take care of the problem,' say some politicians. Officials argue that the country won't be able to export wheat if it is distributed free. They propose exporting the poor instead.

## High-rise parking proposed on land meant for zoo

Fat cats, mall rats, big fish, land sharks and lucky dogs will however be allowed to park.

## Kabul steps in to stop run on biggest bank

'Why can't they keep their money in Swiss banks, like normal people,' asks a peeved minister of finance, chafing at the extra work.

**PM: Let us hope inflation will come down in coming months.**

'But I am no astrologer,' he added, 'and neither am I into tarot cards.' But he did admit a weakness for an arcane branch of voodoo called economics.

**Many ministers declare assets worth only a few lakhs**

'No wonder nobody wants to be a minister,' said a political analyst with a straight face. 'It's no surprise they had to be dragged kicking and screaming to the swearing-in ceremony.'

*Manas Chakravarty in Hindustan Times*

## HEADACHE

Pharmacist to customer: 'In order to buy migraine pills, Sir, you need a proper prescription. A picture of your "wife" is just not enough!'

*Contributed by Vipin Buckshey, New Delhi*

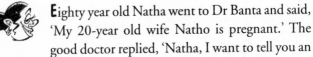

**E**ighty year old Natha went to Dr Banta and said, 'My 20-year old wife Natho is pregnant.' The good doctor replied, 'Natha, I want to tell you an interesting story. Please listen carefully. A hunter went into a forest. Instead of the gun he took his umbrella. He saw a lion and pressed the button of his umbrella and the lion died.'

Natha said, 'Impossible, *kisi aur ne goli mari hogi*' (somebody else might have shot the lion).

'Exactly,' the doctor remarked.

*Contributed by J P Singh Kaka, Bhopal*

## HOME MINISTER, HON'BLE SHRI P. CHIDAMBARAM

**L**et us hope...

He will screw terrorism the way he screwed the economy and brought down the stock market.

~

Introduce service tax on terrorism and fringe benefit tax on NSG.

*Contributed by Vipin Buckshey, New Delhi*

# THE GREAT INDIAN COMMONWEALTH GAMES

Now that so many medals have been won
  And it has been such great fun
Nothing in the matter needs to be done
  Why speak of the misdeeds of OC.

And their alleged loot of the country
  Are Kalmadi and Co not the architects of India's
    sporting history? And our victory!
What have the players, the wrestlers and the shooters
    done?
  It is the organisers who have all the medals won!

Shouldn't the grand opening function
  Put a closure to cases of corruption?
Tickets sold out, stadia empty
  Another feather in the cap of the committee?

And shouldn't the closing ceremony
  Get them Bharat Ratna and some more money?
The government must give them their due
  And make them all governors too.

*Contributed by Kuldip Salil, Delhi*

# DRESS CODE

 Henry Ford II, son of Henry Ford I, who felt that his father was generally improperly dressed and did not adhere to the correct dress code, had the following conversation with him:

*Henry Ford II:* 'Dad, you are the biggest manufacture of cars and a very renowned person in America. Then why do you dress so shabbily?'

*Henry Ford I:* 'Yes, I dress the way I like, as everyone in America knows me as Henry Ford.'

*Henry Ford II:* 'But, when you go abroad, there also you dress in the same way, even in poshest of places.'

*Henry Ford I:* 'Yes, of course, abroad also I dress the same way, because there no one knows me as Henry Ford.'

*Contributed by Col. Trilok Mehrotra, Noida*

# PRAYER

Grant me the senility to forget the people I never liked.
    The good fortune to run into the ones I do,
and the eyesight to tell the difference.

*Contributed by Vipin Buckshey, New Delhi*

## HOLY SPIRIT

Some people turn to God
  Some turn to alcohol
Honestly speaking I don't see any difference,
  Both ways life is being guided by a Spirit.

*Contributed by Vipin Buckshey, New Delhi*

## NOT ALWAYS SAFE

Santa: 'I have heard that using condom is very safe.'

Banta: 'Not at all, I had used it. Still my girl friend's husband beat me up.'

*Contributed by Vinay Asawa, Howrah*


## 'PRESS'

Manoj: 'What happened, *yaar*. You are bandaged up. Did you have an accident?'

Vinod: 'No, I didn't have an accident. Actually I was attending a media function.'

Manoj: 'So how come you got hurt so badly?'

Vinod: 'There was a lady reporter there with a tab on her chest on which it was written 'Press'. So I pressed it.'

*Contributed by Rajeshwari Singh, Delhi*

## BIHARI 'HUMOUR'

**A** Bihari went to a cigarette shop and asked, *'Bhai ek Will dena'*. (Give me a Will.) The shopkeeper told him there is no brand by that name. 'It is Wills,' he said. But the man insisted and said he wanted one Will. The shopkeeper told him that unless he says it correctly; he won't sell it to him. The Bihari went mad and said, *'Hum ek hi to maang rahey hain, poora packet to nahin maang rahey!'* (I am only asking for one cigarette not the whole pack).

*Contributed by K. Bhatia, New Delhi*

## BLACK MONEY

**G**enie meets a Pakistani. Genie to Pakistani: 'Order me, my master. What can I do for you?'

Pakistani: 'Bring me all the wealth in the Swiss banks.'

Genie: 'My name is Genie, not Zardari.'

*Contributed by Rahul Sharma, Gurgaon*

## BONKERS

**D**octor: 'Any history of insanity in the family?'

Lady: 'Yes, my husband thinks he is the Boss.'

*Contributed by Vipin Buckshey, Delhi*

## UP IN SMOKE

 **D**uring Premier Krushchev's visit to America, he presented a box of world famous Havana cigars to President Kennedy, who enjoyed cigars. Though Kennedy accepted the cigars, he later directed his ADC to destroy them as they had come from Fidel Castro's Cuba, a hostile neighbour with whom relations were strained.

A few days later, Kennedy desired to smoke a good cigar and enquired from his ADC, 'Have you done away with the cigars?' The ADC, who too enjoyed smoking the choicest of coronas, faithfully replied to the President, 'Yes, Sir, they have all been burnt, one by one.'

*Contributed by Col. Trilok Mehrotra, Noida*

## HONEYMOON LEAVE

 **P**utting his fist on the application, the boss growled, 'How much leave will you need? Is there no end to your greed?'

'The first time, I took leave for my engagement, the second time, I had to make arrangements and get married,' said the employee.

'And this time, I need a few days' more leave, Sir. Because my wife is going on honeymoon — and she wants me to accompany her.'

*Contributed by Suman Lamba, Cuttack*

## ANNA OR ANATHEMA

My name is Anna Hazare
    And I am crusader with a cause,
The effect of which has given,
    My government a very big toss.
I started my protest with a fast,
    To continue as long as I can last.
My reservations are against
    Corruption, anarchy and bribe
And I resolve to lead this diatribe.
    Unless I can have my final say
And India finally sees that day.
    When every Indian proudly declares
To catch the corrupt unawares.
    I am Anna for the masses
But anathema for our elected bosses.

*Contributed by Sandeep Dewan, Delhi*


## BRIDAL PRAYER

*Rabaa, yaa tay sass changi hovey*
        *nahi-taan photo tangi hovey!*

(Lord, give me a kind mother-in-law.
    If not, let her picture be hanging on the wall).

*Contributed by Vipin Buckshey, New Delhi*

39

**A** man boards a flight from Delhi to Mumbai. As he settles in, he glances up and sees a gorgeous woman boarding the plane. She heads straight towards him and takes the seat next to his. Eager to strike up a conversation, he asks, 'Business trip or vacation?' She smiles and says, 'Business. I'm going to the annual Sexologists convention.' He swallows hard and calmly asks, 'What's your role at this convention?'

'Lecturer,' she says, 'I use my experience to debunk some of the popular myths about sexuality.'

'Really? What m-m-m-m-myths are those?'

'Well,' she explains, 'one popular myth is that African men are the best endowed when, in fact, it's the Tamilians who are most likely to possess that trait. Another popular myth is that Frenchmen are the best lovers, whereas actually it is Bengalis. However, we have found that the best potential lover in all the categories is a Sardar.'

Suddenly, the woman becomes a little uncomfortable and blushes, 'I'm sorry,' she says. 'I shouldn't be discussing this with you. I don't even know your name!'

'Venkatraman!' the man blurts out. 'Venkatraman Mukherjee. But all my friends call me Sardar Joginder Singh.'

*Contributed by Paramjit S Kochar, New Delhi*

# CODE WORD

 **O**n my first posting as a subaltern in 1961, my unit was tasked with construction of the highest airfield in the world at Chushul (14,300 ft), Ladakh. For security reasons, our personal outgoing mail was regularly censored.

Not wishing to share with the censor board the romantic contents of letters to his fiancee, a senior colleague of mine resolved the issue by interjecting a few self-made abbreviations with hidden messages for her. His first abbreviated message to his fiancee read HOLLAND meaning, Hope Our Love Lives And Never Dies.

His frequent requests for compassionate leave were always turned down by the sadistic commanding officer. Finally, when his leave was sanctioned after six months, my desperate friend sent an urgent telegram to his anxiously awaiting, forcibly separated (courtesy the Army) bride of six months, which read — ARRIVING SOON, BURMA.

On his return from leave, with a twinkle in his eyes, he explained the full form of BURMA — Be Undressed Ready My Adorable.

*Contributed by Col. Trilok Mehrotra, Noida*

# FINAL DESTINATION

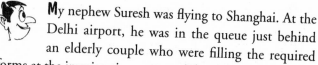 **M**y nephew Suresh was flying to Shanghai. At the Delhi airport, he was in the queue just behind an elderly couple who were filling the required forms at the immigration counter. The wife was asking her husband how to fill the form and he was getting somewhat irritated.

'Port of embarkation' was no problem. She wrote: 'Delhi.'

Next was 'Final destination'. She asked, 'What should I write?' Said the husband, 'Just write Nigambodh Ghat. That will fox them.'

*Contributed by DB Mohindra, New Delhi*


# A PERFECT IDIOT

Mohan: 'I suppose you think I'm a perfect idiot.'

Sohan: 'Oh, none of us is perfect.'

*Contributed by Rajnish Sharma, Shimla*

# IN DEFENCE OF SHASHI T.

Once a good minister from Madras,
　　Stated to be of high taste and class,
Was asked to travel economy
　　He exclaimed: 'Why me!
I do not travel in cattle class.'

Once a suave but naive minister
　　Became victim of a situation so sinister
That he was compelled to bow
　　To the wishes of holy cow;
But on Twitter, his 'tweet' he did register.

A minister was deprived of 5-star
　　On his mind, it did leave a scar.
Where will be my gym?
　　Where will I swim?
This is carrying the matter too far.

*Contributed by J K Mathur, Gurgaon*

# COLOURS OF HOLI

Explaining her aversion to Holi, a woman said, 'My boss is purple with rage at me for coming late to office; my bank balance shows I am green with envy at our neighbours; the rising prices give me the blues; life looks black. Do you think I need more colour in my life?'

*Contributed by Swaran Kaur, New Delhi*

# BUTT OF COURSE

'Fingerprinting is a useful system of biometric identification,' Professor Shigoemi Koshimizu told a press conference at the Advanced Institute of Industrial Technology in Tokyo, '...but fingers are often covered in grease or dirt, which makes fingerprinting unsuitable for mission critical applications. Facial recognition, retina signature and voice recognition also depend on environmental factors, such as lighting or ambient noise, so we have recently developed a new and more versatile form of biometric technology. We call it a "butt fingerprint", and it could soon be used to protect your car against would-be criminals.

'Unlike other biometric technologies, "butt biometrics" does not require any special environmental conditions. We use a seat pressure map to generate a web of 39 indices which identify a subject's buttocks, then embed it in the car driver's seat to prevent carjacking or car theft. If the car doesn't recognise the driver's butt as belonging to its owner the engine stalls. Tests so far have been encouraging, with an error rate of only 1.1%, and the same technology could be used in offices, to automatically log employees on to their computers, or generate a "foot map" as a key for accessing secure rooms or buildings.'

*Contributed by Private Eye, London*

## MIND YOUR LANGUAGE

Lok Sabha Speaker to shouting MPs: 'No unparliamentary language in the House please.'

MP: 'Strange sir! My wife often shouts saying, "No parliamentary language in the house." '

*Contributed by G.S. Rathore, Ludhiana*

## BEING UPPITY

**L**earning the nuances of English makes it a difficult language. But, then, that's probably true of many languages. There is a two-letter word in English that perhaps has more meaning than any other two-letter word, and that word is 'up'. It is listed in the dictionary as being used as an (adv), (pre), (adj), (n), or (v).

It's easy to understand up, meaning toward the sky or at the top of the list, but when we awaken in the morning why do we wake up?

At a meeting, why does a topic come up? Why do we speak up, and why are the officers up for elections and why is it up to the secretary to write up a report?

We call up our friends and we use it to brighten up a room, polish up the silver. We warm up the leftovers and clean up the kitchen. We lock up the house and some guys fix up the old car. At other times, the little word has a real special meaning. People stir up trouble, line up for tickets, work up an appetite, and think up excuses.

To be dressed is one thing but to be dressed up is special.

And this up is confusing:

We open up a store in the morning but we close it up at night. We seem to be pretty mixed up about Up!

To be knowledgeable about the proper use of up, look the word up in the dictionary. In a desk-sized dictionary it takes up almost 1/4th of the page and can add up to about thirty definitions.

If you are up to it, you might try building up a list of the many ways up is used. It will take up a lot of your time, but if you don't give up, you may wind up with a hundred or more. When the sun comes out, we say it is clearing up. When it rains, it wets up the earth. When it does not rain for a while, things dry up.

One could go on and on, but I'll wrap it up for now... my time is up, so time to shut up!

Oh... one more thing: Now I'll shut up.

*Contributed by Vipin Buckshey, New Delhi*

## THREE IMPONDERABLES

If swimming is a good exercise to stay fit, why are whales fat?

Shall I say that there is racial discrimination in chess as the white piece always moves first!!

Why does a round pizza come in a square box?

*Contributed by Charanjeet Singh, Toronto*

## SELECTIVE HEARING

An elderly gentleman had serious hearing problems for many years. He went to the doctor and got himself a set of hearing aids that allowed him to hear 100 per cent. A month later, the doctor remarked, 'Your hearing is perfect. Your family must be really pleased that you can hear again.'

The gentleman replied, 'Oh, I haven't told them. I just sit around and listen to their conversation. I've changed my Will three times.'

*Contributed by Vipin Buckshey, New Delhi*

## JOURNEY

Santa was travelling in a train. A woman sat on his son's berth and didn't get up...

Santa shouted: 'This lady is not giving birth to my child!'

*Contributed by Seema Choudhary, New Delhi*

# TIT FOR TAT

An Iranian walks into a bar in America late one night. An American guy takes the stool beside him.

'Are you one of those "ians"?' asks the American, in a scornful tone. Taken aback, the Iranian asks, 'What do you mean?'

'No difference: Arabian, Iranian, Indian, all the same,' says the American in a slightly insulting tone, laughing out loud.

The Iranian asks instead, 'Are you one of those "keys"?'

'What would that mean?' the American asks.

The Iranian replies, 'No difference: donkey, Yankee, monkey all the same.'

*Contributed by Vipin Buckshey, New Delhi*

# THE ETERNAL QUESTION

Sohan: 'Which came first? The chicken or the egg?'

Mohan: 'Give me the dates on which that particular chicken was hatched, and the date on which the concerned egg was laid, and I will give you the answer.'

*Contributed by Rajeshwari Singh, New Delhi*

## REASON NOT RHYME

The nine-year-old granddaughter of a retired school teacher asked his opinion on her essay. The old man found little to criticise, but he pointed out that it was not considered a good practice to use the same word twice in one sentence if a suitable synonym was available.

How faithfully she followed the advice became evident when she brought home a sample she had made in her English composition class. It read, 'Home Sweet House'.

*Contributed by Reeten Ganguly, Tezpur*

## THE MIGHTY 'E'

One spelling mistake can destroy your life!

A husband wrote a message to his wife on his business trip and forgot to add 'e' at the end of a word...

'I'm having such a wonderful time! Wish you were her...'

*Contributed by Vipin Buckshey, New Delhi*

# SIMPLY PUT

 Indian government has made strenuous efforts to popularise greater use of Hindi over the past several decades. These efforts have, however, not met with much success mainly due to the government's insistence on the use of Sanskritised Hindi, which the common man does not understand, instead of pushing for Hindustani (a mix of Hindi and Urdu), which is the *lingua franca*.

A factual, if somewhat crude; example illustrates this perfectly. When public toilets were first built at the bus stand in Palampur, Himachal Pradesh, the sign at their entrance read: '*Shauchalaya*', which meant conveniences. Since this fancy language went right over the heads of the simple hill folk, they kept on relieving themselves all over the country-side, thus creating a health hazard.

After some months, the local administration, realising their folly, changed the sign to read '*Sandaas*' which means 'toilet'. The local public still did not comprehend and continued following their old ways, irrigating and fertilising the fields.

Finally, in desperation, the authorities changed the signboard again. This time it read '*Tattiyan*' which meant 'place to shit'. This did the trick, and thereafter there were no more cleaning up problems.

*Contributed by Rajeshwari Singh, New Delhi*

## AT THE WRONG END

 **T**wo elderly ladies met every Saturday morning in a cafe to chat and have coffee. One of them was hard of hearing, used a hearing aid and suffered from constipation, requiring glycerine suppositories to clear her bowels. One morning she turned up with a suppository in her ear. She could hardly hear what her friend was saying. The friend shouted: 'Mary, you have a suppository in your ear.'

Mary took it out and replied: 'Now I know where I put my hearing aid.'

*Contributed by Amit Tuteja, Washington D. C.*

## IS GOD DEAF?

**O**ur neighbour has proven religious bearings;
    For public, his *bhajans-keertans* are snaring.
He installs loud-speakers
    For divinity seekers.
As if his gods are a little hard of hearing!!!

*Contributed by J K Mathur, Lucknow*

## MAMA'S CHOICE

**A** young Indian excitedly tells his mother he's fallen in love and is going to get married. He says, 'Just for fun, Ma, I'm going to bring over three girls and you guess which one I'm going to marry.' The mother agrees.

The next day, he brings three beautiful girls and sits them down on the couch. After a while he asks, 'Ma, guess which one I'm going to marry.'

She immediately replies, 'The one on the right.'

'That's amazing. How did you know?'

Mother replies, 'I don't like her.'

*Contributed by Vipin Buckshey, New Delhi*

## A QUESTION OF SALARY

**S**anta was filling up an application form for a job. He was not sure as to what to put in the column 'Salary Expected'.

After much thought he wrote : 'Yes, please.'

*Contributed by Brij Mehra, New Delhi*

**G**od works in mysterious ways.

A woman and a man are involved in a car accident on a snowy, cold Monday morning; it's a bad one. Both their cars are totally demolished, but amazingly neither of them is hurt.

After they crawl out of their cars, the man yells at the woman driver. The woman says, 'So, you're a man. That's interesting. I'm a woman. Wow, just look at our cars! There's nothing left, but we're unhurt. This must be a sign from God that we should be friends and live in peace for the rest of our days.'

Flattered, the man replies, 'Oh yes, I agree completely. This must be a sign from God! But you're still at fault... women should not be allowed to drive.'

The woman continues, 'And look at this, here's another miracle. My car is completely demolished but this bottle of wine didn't break. Surely God wants us to drink this wine and celebrate our good fortune.'

She hands the bottle to the man. The man nods his head in agreement. Opens the bottle, drinks half the bottle and hands it back to the woman.

The woman takes the bottle, puts the cap back on and hands it back to the man.

The man asks, 'Aren't you having any?'

The woman replies, 'No, I think I'll just wait for the police.'

*Contributed by Vipin Buckshey, New Delhi*

## GOD BE PRAISED

 **C**lose friends Santa and Banta met every other day. Once Banta went out of town for a fortnight. As soon as he was back, he went to see his friend. 'So how is it going *yaar?*'

Santa raised his hands skywards and replied, '*Rab dee mehr hai* (thank God, all is well).'

'And how is *bhabhi* (your wife)?' asked Banta

Santa again raised his hands skywards and replied, '*Rab kol challee gayee* (she has gone to God)!'

'What?' asked Banta, 'Why didn't you telephone and tell me?'

Santa replied, 'I wanted to give you a surprise.'

*Contributed by Harjeet Singh, New Delhi*

## RADIO PAKISTAN

**A**salam Alekum, this is Radio Pakistan with today's Sports News:

First we start with the results of tomorrow's cricket match...

*Contributed by Vipin Buckshey, New Delhi*

## ON SEDITION

Freedom comes with restraint
    So we angrily paint
Free speech without permission
    As heinous sedition

In Srinagar, the separatists say
    Whatever they may
But in Delhi, if they utter a word
    Which has been so often heard

And never been found absurd,
    It is fit case for sedition
Because it can break the nation
    It is indeed a tribute to our democracy

That it finds it so risky
    To tolerate dissent,
Motivated or well-meant,
    Because like a cream cake
Which can so easily break
    The unity of the country is at stake

*Contributed by Kuldip Salil, Delhi*


## MAKING APPOINTMENT

Forgiving terrorists is God's job.
    Fixing their appointments with God is our job.

*Contributed by J P Singh Kaka, Bhopal*

**A** shopkeeper went to a barber for a haircut. After the cut he asked about the bill and the barber replied: 'I cannot accept money from you. I'm doing Lok Sewa this week.' The shopkeeper was pleased and thanked him. Next morning the barber found a 'thank you' card and a box of sweets waiting for him at his door.

Later a policeman came in for a haircut, and when he tried to pay his bill, the barber gave the same reply. The cop left happy and the next morning the barber found another card and basket of fruits waiting for him.

The same thing happened with a college professor who came in for a haircut. The next morning, there was a card and a dozen books, including 'How to improve your business'.

Then a member of the Lok Sabha came in for a haircut and when he went to pay his bill, the barber again refused the payment, giving the same reply. The MP was pleased and left.

The next morning when the barber went to open his shop, there were a dozen members of the Lok Sabha lined up waiting for free haircuts.

*Contributed by Vipin Buckshey, New Delhi*

# AN UNLIKELY MATCH

 **A** girl's father is interviewing his would-be son-in-law.

Father: 'Do you smoke?'

Boy: 'Yes, three to four packets a day.'

Father: 'Do you take alcohol?'

Boy: 'Yes, I have four large pegs of rum every evening.'

Father: 'Do you take drugs?'

Boy: 'Yes, I regularly take Ecstasy and sometimes cocaine.'

Father: 'Do you gamble?'

Boy: 'Yes, every weekend, I play *teen-patti* for high stakes.'

Father: 'All negative traits! Is there anything positive about you?'

Boy: 'Yes, HIV.'

*Contributed by Rajeshwari Singh, Delhi*


# EPIGRAMS

The success of a working girl lies in ensuring that the husband doesn't seek solace in the bottle and the baby does.

～

Democracy is a system where the best actor wins not an Oscar but a passage to the legislature.

*Contributed by Jayanti Datta Gupta, Kolkata*

## SMALL-TOWN MILLIONAIRE?

Why is it that *Slumdog Millionaire*
 Stumps me with shame, ennui and fear?
What will they find next worth a million
 In India shining with shades a zillion?
Why is it always Kolkata, Mumbai or Delhi
 That yield hidden treasures so many?
Hey! There you slumped dog-seekers
 Small towns too have their bleaters
And if you kindly excuse my saying folks
 Small holes are birthplaces of lucky slum blokes.
And one for a small-town slumdog millionaire
 Sorry if this slum doggerel is too much to bear.

*Contributed by Sami Rafiq, Aligarh*


## HOBSON'S CHOICE

What do you think of the two candidates for mayor?
Well, I'm glad only one can be elected.

*Contributed by Rajnish Sharma, Shimla*

Cocktail lounge, Norway: Ladies are requested not to have children in the bar.

~

At Budapest Zoo: Please do not feed the animals. If you have any suitable food, give it to the guard on duty.

~

In a Nairobi restaurant: Customers who find our waitresses rude ought to see the manager.

~

Outside a Nairobi school: No trespassing without permission.

~

In a Lima hotel: Open seven days a week, and weekends too.

~

In the lobby of a Moscow hotel across from a Russian Orthodox Monastery: You are welcome to visit the cemetery where famous Russian and Soviet composers, artists, and writers are buried daily except Thursday.

~

The best: In a Beijing bar: Special cocktails for the ladies with nuts.

*Contributed by Vipin Buckshey, New Delhi*

## NO TEETHING TROUBLES

 Banta: 'Santa, I am thinking of making my son an eye-specialist. I am told eye specialists earn a lot of money doing eye-surgery and making spectacles. What do you think?'

Santa: 'I think you should make him a dentist. After all people have only two eyes while they have 32 teeth. So naturally a dentist gets more work.'

*Contributed by J P Singh Kaka, Bhopal*


## TRUE LIES

The husband was late returning from work, so his wife, who was busy cooking asked her six-year-old son to ring Papa's office and find out when he would be home. Ten minutes later the son said that he had telephoned the office several times, but each time a lady came on the line, and he could not get through.

The wife got suspicious and the moment her husband returned home she confronted him about the identity of the girl working late with him. The husband was perplexed as he had been working alone. He called his six-year-old and asked him what the lady on the phone had said. The son replied, 'Each time I phoned, the lady said: "All lines on this route are busy." '

*Contributed by Rajeshwari Singh, New Delhi*

# CHANGING TIMES

Circa 1970: 'Son, please marry a girl from the same caste as us.'

Circa 1980: 'Son, please marry a girl belonging to our religion.'

Circa 1990: 'Son, please marry a girl of our social status.'

Circa 2000: 'Son, please marry a girl from our own country.'

Circa 2010: 'Son, please marry a girl.'

*Contributed by Rajeshwari Singh, New Delhi*


# HURRY OM!

 A Hindu in the US suffered a heart attack on the road and was picked up by an ambulance. Being religious, he kept repeating — *Hari Om, Hari Om, Hari Om.*

When the ambulance pulled into his driveway, his wife came out and screamed to the paramedics, 'Why didn't you take him straight to the hospital?'

'He kept saying hurry home, hurry home!' they replied.

*Contributed by Paramjit S Kochar, New Delhi*

# SARCASTIC SMILES

I smile when

Prakash Karat says, 'Excuse me I am extremely blunt,
    My party is neither with Congress nor with BJP
        We want to forge a third front.'

L.K. Advani says, 'Being a humble man I don't boast,
    I have an unfulfilled desire I simply covet PM's post.'

Mayawati says, 'My birthday bash enacted a wonderful
        scene,
    The topmost Babus of Uttar Pradesh adored me like a
        Phantom Queen.'

Our maid-servant says, 'Sir, the day is not very far,
    When to render domestic help I shall come to your house
        in a Nano car.'

*Contributed by G C Bhandari, Meerut*


# QUICK FIX

Santa joined NASA.

After one month the Americans had to change the name from NASA to SATYANASA.

*Contributed by Brij Mehra, New Delhi*

# LIE DETECTOR TEST

 **R**ohan was fed up with his son Amit, who was lying all the time. So he persuaded a scientist friend to make a robot which would slap anyone who told lies in its presence. Rohan took the robot home and kept it in his study. One day Amit came very late from school. So Rohan and his wife Meeta took the boy into the former's study in order to question him.

Rohan: 'Why are you so late?'

Amit: 'Our teacher was taking extra classes.' (The robot immediately went up to Amit and gave him a slap.)

Amit: 'Actually, I went to see a movie.'

Rohan: 'Which movie?'

Amit: '*Jai Hanuman.*' (The robot gave him another slap.)

Amit: 'Actually, it was *Red Hot Nights.*'

Rohan: 'When I was your age son, I never told lies.'

The robot turned around, moved immediately to Rohan and gave him a slap. Seeing this, his wife spoke up, 'No wonder he tells lies. After all, he's your son.'

The robot at once moved over to Meeta, and slapped her.

*Contributed by Rajeshwari Singh, New Delhi*

## IT'S ALL ABOUT MONEY!

 **O**ne day, many years ago at a school in South London, a teacher said to a class of ten-year-olds, 'I'll give £20 to the child who can tell me who was the most famous man who ever lived?'

An Irish boy said, 'It was St Patrick.' The teacher said 'Sorry Alan, that's wrong'.

A Scottish boy, 'It was St Andrew.' 'That is not right either,' the teacher replied.

Finally Jayant, son of a Gujarati trader, said, 'Jesus Christ.' 'That is right, Jayant,' said the teacher. After giving Jayant £20 the teacher said, 'You are Gujarati, and you gave the correct answer. I am so surprised.' Jayant replied, 'Yes, in my heart I knew it was Lord Krishna, but business is business.'

*Contributed by Vipin Buckshey, New Delhi*

## TEACHING ANTONYMS

**M**y friend was teaching his four-year old grandson. There was the word 'hardship' in the book. So my friend with full earnest efforts tried to explain the exact meaning. 'You know Sonny,' he said, 'hardship means severe suffering, trouble etc.'

The little boy listened carefully. After a minute, he calmly asked, 'Grandpa, is there any word called softship?'

*Contributed by Reeten Ganguly, Tezpur*

## THE GOLDEN CUP

Beaming, booming, bursting
    Dancing wild with joy, with tails up
Hurrah: We have won the World Cup
    Night turns into day and the day into eternity
For once casteless, creedless with just Indian identity
    A billion plus people become a fraternity.
Ah this rarest of the rare unity,
    A madness in which every beggar is a king.
And from coast to coast Indian is the world's toast
    Is it not time now that everything else should go to hell
And we eat cricket, drink cricket and live under its spell
    Time that with wealth and glory
These heroes are fed so wantonly
    That they become two quintals fat and ten feet tall
And into a lengthy slumber fall!

*Contributed by Kuldip Salil, Delhi*


## INSTANT ROMANCE

The shortest romance in the world: 'He tried, she sighed, baby cried'.

*Contributed by Andy Nunes, Goa*

# Q.E.D.

**A** representative from India at the UN Assembly began his address thus: 'Before beginning my talk I want to tell you something about Rishi Kashyap of Kashmir, after whom Kashmir is named. When Rishi Kashyap struck a rock and it brought forth water, he thought, "What a good opportunity to have a bath." He took off his clothes, put them aside on the rock and entered the water. When he got out and wanted to dress, his clothes had vanished. A Pakistani had stolen them.'

The Pakistani representative jumped up furiously and shouted, 'What are you talking about? The Pakistanis weren't there then.'

The Indian smiled and said, 'And now that we have made that clear, I will begin my speech saying that Kashmir has been an integral part of India all along.'

*Contributed by Vipin Buckshey, New Delhi*

## TAKING GUARD

**T**he first testicular guard was used in cricket in 1874. The first helmet was used in 1974.

It took cricketers a hundred years to discover that their brains are as important as their private parts.

*Contributed by Amarinder Bajaj, New Delhi*

## WRONG SELECTION

 **A** pretty young girl was kidnapped by a gang of dacoits. She was tied up and the gang leader approached her menacingly.

Girl (screaming): 'Don't you dare touch me. I am a married woman.'

Gang leader: 'You need not worry, sister, your honour is safe. I am gay. If only those stupid men of mine had kidnapped your husband, instead of you!'

*Contributed by Rajeshwari Singh, New Delhi*


## ROYAL PICK

**A** young man was being interviewed for a job as a salesman in an antique store. The owner picked up a chip of wood from the floor, put it on a red velvet cushion and asked, 'What's that?'

'Emperor Akbar's toothpick.'

'Excellent, you can start right away.'

*Contributed by Reeten Ganguly, Tezpur*

# IN VINO VERITAS

**A** guru was trying to convince his *chela* about giving up alcohol since it was not only injurious to health but was also destroying his family life. The *chela* then turned to a greater force for his defence.

*Gin mein basi hai Janki*
*Rum mein basay hain Ram*
*Whiskey mein Vishnu basey*
*Thharre mein Hanuman*
*Sab main hai Bhagwan basey*
*Toh kisko chhodoon Ram*
*Jai Patiala, Jai Shri Ram!*

*Contributed by Kamlaji Jagdish, Kanpur*

# TOURISM

**F**aithful husbands will go straight to Heaven and unfaithful will enjoy Heaven on Earth...!!

The choice is yours.

*Contributed by Vipin Buckshey, New Delhi*

## AN AFGHAN MOTHER'S PRAYER

 The following verse based on Hans Anderson's fairy tale character Thumbelina — size of a thumb — was scribbled on a card by the novelist-poet Tabish Khair when he paid me a visit in Delhi. He is now living in Anderson's country Denmark where he teaches English in Aarthus University:

Grant me a little child I can hide.
    When the Mullahs come home to pray,
Someone, smaller than my thumb;
    I can put in my pocket and run.

*Contributed by Khushwant Singh, New Delhi*

## POST SCRIPT

There is a cinema hall in Amritsar which has closed down. The last film screened in it was *Agar Tum Na Hotey*.

Years after it had closed down the name of the film remained painted on its boundary wall. Below the film's title somebody wrote *'Yeh cinema band na hota'*!

*Contributed by K J S Ahluwalia, Amritsar*

## SEEN ON AN EXAMINATION PAPER

General Students: Answer all questions.

OBCs: Answer any one question.

SCs: Only read questions.

STs: Thanks for coming.

Gujjars: Thanks for allowing others to attend the examination!!

*Contributed by Vipin Buckshey, New Delhi*

## SUPER SPECIALISTS

A doctor is a person who kills your ills with his pills, and you with his bills.

~

A gynaecologist is one who looks for problems, at places where others look for pleasure.

*Contributed by Amrinder Bajaj, Delhi*

## OUR CRICKETING HEROES

On hard, dry, lifeless tracks
    Our batsmen their willows smack
Cut, chop, drive, hook, pull and punch
    Not till 600+ are they done
I pity the poor old cricket ball
    On grassy, bouncy, swinging strips
Alas! Their ability dips
    Their leaden bodies and clay feet
Can't prevent ball and stumps meet
    The team's score like a telephone number
In search of glory
    They create a world record 20 overs for an entire
        innings!
Don't blame the coach
    He's not playing on the field.
Who is to blame?
    No one. For you see
It's a game of uncertainty.

*Contributed by Nicholas Koch, Delhi*

## CHINESE PUZZLE

A Chinese couple named Mr and Mrs Hua were actually not married when they had a pair of twins. They put down their names as Jo Hua, So Hua.

*Contributed by J P Singh Kaka, Bhopal*

## TILL DEATH DO US PART...

An elderly gentleman was invited to an old friend's home for dinner. He was impressed by the way his friend preceded every request to his wife with endearing terms such as Honey, My love, Darling, Sweetheart, Pumpkin, etc.

The couple had been married almost 70 years and clearly they were still very much in love. While the wife was in the kitchen, the man leaned over and said to his host, 'I think it's wonderful that, after all these years, you still call your wife those loving pet names.'

The old man hung his head, 'I have to tell you the truth,' he said. 'Her name slipped my mind about 10 years ago and I'm scared to death to ask her what it is.'

*Contributed by Vipin Buckshey, New Delhi*

## MODEL–T

Santa: 'What is the name of your car?'

Banta: 'I forgot the name, but it starts with 'T'.'

Santa: 'Oh, what a strange car, starts with tea. All cars that I know start with petrol.'

*Contributed by Gaurav Shah, Surat*

# WRONG NUMBER

 **R**eturning from a *theka*, Santa says to Banta, 'I can't walk all the way home.'

'I know,' says Santa, 'but we have no money for a cab and we've missed the last bus.'

'We could steal a bus from the depot,' Santa suggests. Banta agrees.

They reach the bus depot and Santa tells Banta to go in and get a bus while he keeps a look-out. After shuffling around for ages, Santa shouts, 'Banta, what are you doing? Have you not found a bus yet?'

Banta shouts, 'I can't find a No. 91.'

Santa: 'You dim-wit, take the No. 14 and we'll walk from the roundabout.'

*Contributed by Vipin Buckshey, New Delhi*


# CHECKMATED

**S**een outside a shop.

'Customer is King. The King never bargains'.

*Contributed by Reeten Ganguly, Tezpur*

## GENERATION GAP

**M**y neighbour's twelve-year-old skinny and lanky son needed a new shirt. He and his wife took him to a shopping mall and the search began. In the boys' department the largest size was too small. They moved to the men's department where the smallest size was too big.

With the largest boys' size in one hand and the smallest men's size in the other, my neighbour's wife gave her son a long look. 'Son,' she said at last, 'do you realise you are now in the generation gap?'

*Contributed by Reeten Ganguly, Tezpur*

## TAAREY ZAMEEN PAR

*Taarey zameen par,*
*Keemtein aasmaan par.*

~

Q: What should be the new name of Twenty 20?
A: Four 20!

*Contributed by K J S Ahluwalia, Amritsar*

# MUSTARD OIL

 **A** customer asked, 'In what aisle could I find the *sarson da tel* (mustard oil)?'

The clerk says, 'You a Sardar?'

The guy clearly offended says, 'Yes, I am. But let me ask you something. If I had asked for Italian olive oil, would you ask me if I was Italian?

'Or if I had asked for German bratwurst, would you ask me if I was German?

'Or if I asked for a kosher hot dog, would you ask me if I was Jewish?

'Or if I had asked for a taco, would you ask if I was Mexican?

'Or if I asked for some Irish whiskey, would you ask if I was Irish?'

The clerk says, 'No, I probably wouldn't.'

The guy says, 'Well, then, because I asked for *sarson da tel,* why did you say I am a Sardar?'

The clerk replied, 'Because you're in a liquor store.'

*Contributed by Vipin Buckshey, New Delhi*

# ANTI CORRUPTION DAY

What did you say: Anti-Corruption Day?
    Don't be silly yaar; you must be joking.
Why do you dig up the archaic word: Anti,
    Spoiling the cocktail of my morning tea,
Flavour of Darjeeling,
    Aroma of corruption,
Fomented by glaring media headlines?
    Your crawling out of mother's belly
Is not enough to prove you are born;
    It needs a proof acquired with bribe.
You pay donation to get admission
    For that fake passport, education,
Then secure a job by greasing palms,
    You don't know, of how many persons.
A licence, a permit, a ration card,
    A bed in a public ward or even a place
In the endless queue of life,
    If you want, You'll get it — only pay the price.
And when this mortal journey is over,
    Don't think you can exit life unnoticed,
You still need proof with a price tag, too.
    Why do you bother and tear your hair?
It is a sore that will fester, stink every day,
    Bringing down the system with its load or explode,
Paving the way for a new order.

*Contributed by A K Das, Lucknow*

# WHAT'S IN A NAME?

**H**ore is a Bengali surname. Poornima Hore (not her real name), a pretty and meritorious girl got a scholarship from an American university. She applied for passport. In the passport office her surname which is pronounced as 'Whore' created rapture among the officials. While she was being interviewed in the American embassy for visa, the middle-aged American officer hearing her surname blushed and with great difficulty checked a guffaw. She felt humiliated.

Subsequently, she reached America and joined the university. But her daily embarrassment with the surname continued. She met a young Bengali engineer who had settled there. He was a bachelor. To get rid of her surname she desperately roped him and breaking the age-old taboo she proposed. After a brief courtship they were married. Now she is known as Poornima H Chatterjee.

*Contributed by Reeten Ganguly, Tezpur*

# BREAKING NEWS!

**I**t has been conveyed by knowledgable sources that Manmohan Singh is planning to write his autobiography. It has been provisionally titled:

3 Mistakes of My Life: 2G, CWG and Sonia G.

## FINALITIES

The differences between complete and finished are:

When you marry the right one, you are complete...

And when you marry the wrong one, you are finished...

And when the right one catches you with the wrong one... then you are completely finished!

*Contributed by Vipin Buckshey, New Delhi*

## GOD VERSUS SATAN

God's plan made a hopeful beginning,
  But man spoilt his chances by sinning,
We know that the story,
  Will end in God's glory,
But at present the other side's winning.

*Contributed by Karan Singh, New Delhi*

## PUSHING A DRUNK

 **A** couple is awakened by pounding on their front door. The man opens the door and finds a drunken stranger standing in the rain. He snarls at the drunk, 'What do you want?'

The drunk slurs, 'Can you give me a push?'

'Not a chance,' says the house owner. 'It's three o'clock in the morning!' He slams the door and returns to bed.

'Who was it?' asks the wife. 'Some drunk asking for a push,' he answers.

'Did you help him?'

'No, it's 3 a.m. and raining like hell!'

'You have a short memory,' says the wife. 'Remember when our car broke down and two strangers helped us? You should help this poor man.'

The husband goes out in the pounding rain, and calls out in the dark, 'Hey, are you there?'

'Yes,' comes the reply.

'Do you still want a push?'

'Yes, please!'

Unable to see anything in the dark, the husband asks, 'Where are you?'

'Over here, on the swing,' replies the drunk.

*Contributed by Rajeshwari Singh, Delhi*

## LAST SUPPER

Three friends Hari Bhai, Sundaram and Santa were doing construction work on a scaffolding on the 20th floor of a building. At lunch time they sat down together with their lunch boxes.

Hari Bhai said, '*Dhokla*! If I get *dhokla* one more time for lunch, I'm going to jump off this building.'

Sundaram opened his lunch box and exclaimed, '*Idli sambhar* again! If I get *idli sambhar* one more time I'm going to jump off too.'

Santa opened his lunch box and said, '*Parantha* again! If I get a *parantha* one more time, I'm jumping too.'

The next day Hari Bhai opened his lunch box, saw *dhokla*, and jumped to his death. Sundaram opened his lunch, saw *idli-sambhar*, and jumped too. Santa opened his lunch, saw the *parantha* and jumped to his death as well.

At the funeral, Hari Bhai's wife was weeping. She said, 'If I'd known how really tired he was of *dhokla*, I never would have given it to him again!' Sundaram's wife also wept and said, 'I could have given him *dosa*! I didn't realise he hated *idli sambhar* so much.'

Everyone turned and stared Santa's wife. She said, 'Don't look at me. He always made his own lunch.'

*Contributed by Vipin Buckshey, New Delhi*

## ALICE IN INDIAN WONDERLAND

 **W**orried about whether the government is following the right policies?

Just remember what the Cheshire Cat told Alice, 'If you don't know where you are going, any road will get you there.'

The government knows this, which is why its mind is completely at rest.

*Contributed by Karan Thapar, New Delhi*

## WHAT IS YOUR MOBILE NUMBER?

**S**anta bought a new mobile. He called everyone in his phone book and told them: 'My mobile number has changed, earlier it was Nokia 3310, now it is 6710.'

*Contributed by Joseph Wasto, Imphal*

## EVE'S DROPPING

'Dear mother-in-law, don't try to tell me how to raise my children. I am married to one of yours and believe me, there is room for improvement.

*Contributed by Amrinder Bajaj, Delhi*

## WOMEN POWER

 We have quite a few women wielding power in national politics. There is Jayalalithaa in Tamil Nadu, Uma Bharati in Madhya Pradesh, Mamata Bannerjee in West Bengal, Mayawati in Uttar Pradesh and Mehbooba Mufti in Kashmir.

There are also Sadhvi Rithambara and Sadhvi Pragya Thakur. Have they anything in common? I can think of one common factor: all of them are single.

You don't have to be a psychologist to infer that they are missing out on something vital in life that accounts for their eccentric behaviour.

*Contributed by Ratan Jain, Pune*

## WARDROBE MAL-FUNCTION

On the ramp, a model in her full gear,
    Forgot to put on her under-wear
When she got exposed
    The crowd was disposed,
To all-round cheers and no jeers!!!

*Contributed by J K Mathur, Lucknow*

# O JERUSALEM!

 **A** man and his wife went on a vacation to Jerusalem. While they were there in the Holy Land, the wife passed away.

The undertaker told the husband, 'You can have her body shipped home for $5,000, or you can bury her here, in the Holy Land, for $150.'

The man thought about it awhile, and told the undertaker, he would just have his wife's remains shipped home.

The undertaker asked, 'Why would you spend $5,000 to ship your wife back home, when it would be wonderful to be buried here, and you would spend only $150?'

The man replied, 'A long time ago, a man called Jesus Christ died here. He was buried here. Three days later He rose from the dead. I just can't take that chance.'

*Contributed by Sonia Khanna, Guwahati*


# TESTING TIMES

 **S**anta's aged mother was ill. The doctor examined the old lady and told Santa, 'I am sorry I will have to put her through more tests.'

Santa was dismayed and said, 'But doctor *sahib*, how can you put her through tests. She is illiterate and can't read or write.'

*Contributed by Col. Trilok Mehrotra, Noida*

## PRIME MINISTER-IN-WAITING

I'm glad Advani will remain the leader of the opposition
    Because he has not yet fulfilled his ambition
Which is, to raise Congress tally to three hundred and one
    I have great respect for Advani, the person
Of intelligence, sharp and articulate
    A man at eighty-one with such a stamina great
And such a good planner and so little a hypocrite
    That from Somnath to Ayodhya, he kindles communal
      strife
And calls Babri demolition 'the saddest day of my life'
    He praised Jinnah because he had an open mind
And applauds Modi because he is one of his own kind
    Undoubtedly the tallest man after Atalji
He would leave behind a feuding BJP
    In which one of the contenders for the *gaddi*
Would be Varun Gandhi.

*Contributed by Kuldip Salil, Delhi*


## REMEMBERING THE MAHATMA

Question: To what extent does our concern for Bapu Gandhi
go today?

Answer: Upto his 'Samadhi' twice a year.

*Contributed by K J S Ahluwalia, Amritsar*

## HUBBY HOWLER

'You are the bravest woman of the land,
   Daring the darkness you took a heroic stand.
We couldn't have got the burglar.
   Hadn't you maimed him with a tumbler.'

'A burglar? Sorry, I thought it was my husband.'

*Contributed by Jayanti Datta Gupta, Calcutta*


## BEHIND SCHEDULE

A man is standing on the road beneath a building and looking up curiously as if he is waiting for something.

A passerby asks him, 'What are you waiting for?'

The man says, 'I am waiting for my watch to arrive. I accidentally dropped it from the 5th floor.'

Passerby, 'But it would have fallen by now.'

The man, 'No, the watch is ten minutes late.'

*Contributed by Anhad Madan, Beas*

# Share a joke with
# Khushwant Singh

If you have a joke, a humorous anecdote or a funny incident, which is original and you would like to share it with Khushwant Singh and his millions of admirers, send it to us today. If selected, it could be printed in the next edition of *Khushwant Singh's Joke Book*.

**Remember**

- Each joke or anecdote must be neatly typed or written on a separate sheet of paper in about 125-150 words.

- Do not type or write on both sides of the sheet. Write on one side only.

- Send your jokes to:

    *Khushwant Singh's Joke Book*
    c/o Orient Paperbacks
    5A/8 Ansari Road,
    NEW DELHI-110 002
    or e-mail to jokes@orientpaperbacks.com

- Each contribution received would be acknowledged.

- Each selected contribution would be acknowledged and included in the next edition of *Khushwant Singh's Joke Book* along with the name of the contributor.

**Khushwant Singh's Joke Book**

Entry Coupon

Name: ......................................................................................

Address: ..................................................................................

..................................................................................

City ...................................Pin ..............................

Each entry must be accompanied by one coupon

- - ✂ - - - - - - - - - - - - - - - - - - - - - - - - - - - -

**Khushwant Singh's Joke Book**

Entry Coupon

Name: ......................................................................................

Address: ..................................................................................

..................................................................................

City ...................................Pin ..............................

Each entry must be accompanied by one coupon

- - ✂ - - - - - - - - - - - - - - - - - - - - - - - - - - - -

**Khushwant Singh's Joke Book**

Entry Coupon

Name: ......................................................................................

Address: ..................................................................................

..................................................................................

City ...................................Pin ..............................

Each entry must be accompanied by one coupon

Women's styles may change, but their designs remain the same.

Running into debt doesn't bother me, it's running into creditors that's upsetting.

Two feet on the ground are worth one in the mouth.

Bachelor: A rolling stone that gathers no moss.

Race horse: An animal that can take several people for a ride at the same time.

A secret: Something you tell only to one person at a time.

A will: A rich man died and a line in his will read 'I leave to my beloved son all the money he owes me.'

What Sheikh Saadi said: I fear the following two: *Rabb, te jahre rabb kolon nahin dardey.* God and those who don't fear the God.

*Contributed by Rajnish, Shimla*

## A STANDPOINT

As a tipping point
    The three-year glitch
Replaces the seven-year itch.
    In the fast paced 21$^{st}$ century
Endless squabbles over nothings,
    Perennial stinginess, weight-gain,
Incessant disturbing snoring,
    Are a few of the passion killers.
A recent survey of adults
    In steady relationships
Highlights the 36-month marker
    When ties of kinship reach the zenith of stress levels.
All this points to a new trend —
    Heading off to solo holidays.
Within a run-down relationship
    An individual gaze into space is presently the
        touchstone.

*Contributed by R P Chadda, Chandigarh*


## DONATE GENEROUSLY

Terrorists have kidnapped our beloved Zardari and are demanding $5,00,000 or they will burn him with petrol. Please donate what you can. I have donated five litres.

*Contributed by S. Rizvi, Lahore*

## POLICE CHASE

**A** beggar is sitting on an Islamabad footpath. Suddenly, the President's motorcade goes past at high speed. A few minutes pass. The beggar just looks on vacantly.

Then a very fat bank robber runs past slowly, clutching a heavy sack of money, wheezing from the effort.

A few more minutes pass. The beggar just gazes on.

Two policemen arrive huffing and puffing. 'Did you see a fat thief pass this way?' they ask the beggar.

'Yes, but you'll never catch him on foot.'

*Contributed by M.N. Rao, Lahore*

## TRY THIS!

**T**ranslate from Hindi to English:

*Khushi ke mare uski chhaati phool gayi.*

Santa: Due to happiness, his chest became breast.

*Contributed by Shruti Garg, Ludhiana*

# HIS LAST WISH

 The Pope lay dying in the hospital. For years he had faithfully served the people of the world. He motioned for his nurse to come near. 'Yes, Father?' said the nurse. 'I would really like to see Asif Zardari and Nawaz Sharif before I die,' whispered the priest.

'I'll see what I can do, Father,' replied the nurse. The nurse sent the request to them and waited for a response.

Soon the word arrived. Zardari and Nawaz Sharif would be delighted to visit the Pope.

As they went to the hospital, Nawaz commented to Zardari 'I don't know why the old man wants to see us, but it will certainly help our images.'

Zardari couldn't help but agree. When they arrived in the Pope's room, the Pope took Zardari's hand in his right hand and Nawaz Sharif's hand in his left. There was silence and a look of serenity on the old Pope's face.

Finally Nawaz spoke, 'Holy Father, of all the people you could have chosen, why did you choose us to be with you as you near the end?'

The old Pope slowly replied, 'I have always tried to pattern my life after our Lord and Saviour, Jesus Christ.' The old priest continued... 'He died between two lying thieves. I would like to do the same.'

*Contributed by Mohd. Iqbal, Lahore*

# THE LAST LAUGH

During vacations some college boys from south India came to Delhi. They rented a taxi for sight-seeing. The driver was an old Sardarji and boys being boys, they began cracking Sardar jokes, just to tease the old man.

To their surprise, the old fellow remained unperturbed.

At the end of the sight-seeing tour, they paid the cab hire charges. The Sardar returned the change and he gave each one of them a ten rupee note extra and said, 'Sons, since morning you have been telling Sardar jokes. I listened to them all and let me tell you, some of them were in bad taste. Still, I don't mind because I know that you are young and are yet to see the world.

'But I have one request. I am giving you ten rupees each. Give it to the first Sardar beggar that you come across in this or any other city. Years later, one of the group of boys recounts, "That ten-rupee note is still with me. I could not find a single Sardar begging anywhere." ' Sikhs contribute: 33% of total income tax 67% of total charities 45% of the Indian Army 59,000 plus gurudwaras serve langar, free of charge, to over 60 lakh people every day! And all this when Sikhs form only 1.4% of the Indian population.

*Contributed by Vijendra Gupta, New Delhi*

## A PEN IS MIGHTIER...

 **A** businessman gave his secretary a costly pen for her birthday. Next morning, she sent him an e-mail which the businessman's wife read.

The e-mail said: 'Your pen is wonderful. I enjoyed using it last night.' Unfortunately, she forgot to put a space between 'pen' and 'is'.

*Contributed by Rajeshwari, Delhi*


## LOYALTY TEST

**A** wife buys a dozen underwear of the same colour for her husband.

Husband: 'Why the same colour? People will think I never change underwear.'

Wife: 'Which people?'

Total silence.

*Contributed by Anusha Dayal, Gujrat*

## SEX STARVED

This happened in 1979 while I was doing a short term *locum* (a temporary substitute) job as Senior House Officer in Obstetrics & Gynaecology in Colchester, England.

In the delivery room, the consultant obstetrician had delivered the baby, clamped the umbilical cord with the forceps, and was patiently waiting for the placenta (afterbirth) to be delivered.

The new mother, a young woman, and her boy friend who was sitting next to her providing her physical and emotional support, suddenly asked the doctor with great urgency and curiosity, 'Doctor, how soon can I have sex with my beloved?'

In a very relaxed manner, looking in young father's eyes the doctor replied, 'Usually people wait until the placenta is delivered.'

*Contributed by Dr. Azad S. Guron, Canada*


## PROFESSIONALISM

Santa was a photographer by profession. On Banta's death he was called. As a matter of habit he went upto the body, adjusted his camera and said, 'Smile, please.'

*Contributed by Dr. N N Laha, Gwalior*

# SUPER POWER SUMMIT

**O**nce God got very upset with all the wars and chaos in the world. He summoned the heads of United States, United Kingdom and Soviet Union in person in his court, and asked them for an explanation as to why they had created so much unrest and chaos in the world.

The US President said, 'God, we follow you, we worship you, all we want from you is that the Soviet Union should be removed from the world map and we promise that there will not be any trouble in the world any more.'

It was the turn of the President of Soviet Union, 'God, we are atheist, we are communists, we don't follow you, but we will start following you, worshipping you, if you can wipe out United States from the world. If you do so, we promise that thereafter there will be peace in the world.'

After listening to the United States and Soviet Union's arguments, God asked the Queen of United Kingdom what did she want.

'God, we have no demand. If you can just fulfil the demands of United States and Soviet Union, our wish (desire) will be automatically fulfilled.'

*Contributed by Dr. Azad S. Guron, Canada*

A dentist to Manmohan Singh during his annual check up: 'Mr Prime Minister, at least in my clinic please open your mouth.'

**A** baby camel asks his mother, 'Mom why have I got these huge three-toed feet?'

The mother replies, 'Well son, when we trek across the desert your toes will help you to stay on top of the soft sand.'

'OK,' replies the son and goes away, but comes back to ask, 'But Mom, why have I got these great long eyelashes?'

'They are there to keep the sand out of your eyes on the trips through the desert.'

After a short while, the son returns and asks, 'Mom why have I got this great big hump on my back?'

The mother replies, 'It is there to help us store water for our long treks across the desert, so we can go without drinking for long periods.'

'That's great mom, so we have huge feet to stop us sinking, and long eyelashes to keep the sand from our eyes and a hump to store water, but... Mom?

'Yes son?'

'Why the heck are we in the Nandankanan Zoo?'

*Contributed by Arivalur V Nagarajan, Chennai*

## PROUD FATHER

Santa: 'I am most proud to tell you that my son is in medical college.'

Banta: 'Really, what is he studying?'

Santa: 'He is not studying, they are studying him.'

*Contributed by Ajay Satpathy, Cuttack*

## ETHICAL BEHAVIOUR

Santa: 'I didn't sleep all night on the train.'

Banta: 'Why?'

Santa: 'I had an upper berth.'

Banta: 'Why didn't you exchange it?'

Santa: 'There was nobody in the lower berth to change it with.'

*Contributed by Shruti Kanitkar, Nagpur*

## INTERNATIONAL TALENT

*In Heaven:*

The cooks are French,
     The policemen are English,
The mechanics are German,
     The lovers are Italian,
The bankers are Swiss.

*In Hell:*

The cooks are English,
     The policemen are German,
The mechanics are French,
     The lovers are Swiss,
The bankers are Italian.

*Contributed by Arati Talwar, Chandigarh*


## MISSING

Lady to Inspector Santa: 'My husband went out to buy potatoes five days ago, he hasn't returned yet!'

Inspector: 'Why don't you cook something else?'

*Contributed by Pragya Sharma, Jabalpur*

# THE ART OF SMUGGLING

**S**anta rides up to the Pakistan border on his bike. He's got two large bags over his shoulders.

The ranger guard Iqbal stops him and asks, 'What's in the bags?'

'Sand,' answers Santa.

'We'll just see about that. Get off the bike.'

Iqbal takes the bags and rips them apart, he empties them out and finds nothing in them but sand. He detains Santa all night and has the sand analysed, only to discover that there is nothing but pure sand in the bags. Iqbal releases Santa, puts the sand into new bags, lifts them onto Santa's shoulders, and lets him cross the border.

A week later, the same thing happens. Iqbal asks, 'What have you got?'

'Sand,' says Santa.

Iqbal does his thorough examination and discovers that the bags contain nothing but sand. He gives the sand back to Santa, who crosses the border on his bike.

This sequence of events is repeated every week for three years. Finally, Santa doesn't show up for several weeks and then the guard, Iqbal chances to meets him at a *dhaba*.

'Oye, Santa,' says Iqbal, 'I know you have been smuggling something. It's driving me crazy. It's all I think about... I can't sleep. Just between you and me, what are you smuggling.'

Santa sips his *lassi* and says, 'Bikes'.

*Contributed by Col. Hardip Judge. Ambala*

# CREATIVE SANTA

Trips over a cordless phone.

Thinks socialism means partying.

Studies for a blood test and fails.

Puts lipstick on his forehead because he wants to make up his mind.

Takes a ruler to bed to see how long he slept.

At the bottom of the application form where it says: 'Sign Here', he puts 'Scorpio'.

Misses the 44 route number bus, and takes the 22 route number twice instead.

Drives to the airport and sees a sign that said, 'Airport left', he turns around and goes home.

Gets locked in furniture shop and sleeps on the floor.

*Contributed by P Subramanium, Trichy*

## ACID TEST

Teacher: 'What is the difference between a problem and a challenge?'

Student: '1 bed, 3 boys, 1 girl — a problem; 1 bed, 3 girls, 1 boy — a challenge.'

*Contributed by Amarinder Bajaj, Delhi*

## FAIL SAFE

Two suicide bombers were fixing a bomb in a car.

'What would you do if the bomb explodes while fixing?' asked one, from the other.

'Don't worry, I have one more,' came the prompt reply.

*Contributed by Col. Hardip Judge, Ambala*

## IN ONE PIECE

Boss: 'Where were you born?'

Santa: 'India.'

Boss: 'Which part?'

Santa: 'What "which part"? The whole body was born in India.'

*Contributed by Sahi, Jamshedpur*

## YOGA THERAPY

 **M**y friend's son Golu used to bite his nails. I advised my friend to send Golu to Baba Ramdev to learn yoga.

After two months I asked my friend, 'How is Golu now?' My friend said, 'Now Golu can bite his toe nails also.'

*Contributed by J P Singh Kaka, Bhopal*


## CONSOLING...

**A**t the scene of an accident a man was crying: 'O God! I have lost my hand, oh!'

Santa: 'Control yourself. Don't cry. See that man. He has lost his head… Is he crying?'

*Contributed by Bilal Khan, Siliguri*


## REWARDING INVESTMENT

**W**ife to her fat husband: You are my only investment that has doubled.

*Contributed by Balram Yadav, Haryana*

# CURTAIN CALL

 **S**anta enters a shop that sells curtains. He announces to the salesman, 'I would like to buy a pair of green curtains.'

Salesman Banta assures him that they have a large selection of green curtains and shows him several patterns, but Santa seems to be having a hard time choosing.

Finally, he selects a striking green floral print. Banta asks him the size of the curtains he requires.

Santa replies, 'Fifteen inches.'

'Fifteen inches?' exclaimed Banta. 'That is a very small curtain. What room size are they for?'

Santa tells him that they aren't for a room, they are for his computer monitor.

An extremely surprised Banta replies, 'But, sir, computers do not need curtains!'

Santa says, 'Helllloooooooooo........ I've got Windows.'

*Contributed by Krishan Lal, Ferozpur*

## PRICE RISE

**A** rich and miserly resident of a posh colony went out for his morning walk. He saw his milkman on a cycle with the milk cans. He asked him to stop. The milk man got down from his cycle. 'Why have you increased the price of milk so drastically?' asked the rich miser.

The milkman said, '*Sahab*, we often hear and watch on TV about water-pollution and its dangerous effects. Considering the health-care of our VIP customers, we, the milkmen in this neighbourhood, decided that we must not mix the tap water with milk anymore. The municipal board's water may contain germs. So we started mixing mineral water. That's why the price rise.'

*Contributed by Reeten Ganguly, Tezpur*

## WHO IS RESPONSIBLE?

**A** man frantically calls the hotel manager from his hotel room. 'Please come at once, I am arguing with my wife and she is threatening to jump out of the window.'

The manager responded, 'Sir, that's a personal matter.'

The guest responded, 'The window won't open! That's a maintenance matter!'

*Contributed by Vipin Buckshey, New Delhi*

# BAPTISM

An Irishman is stumbling through the woods, totally drunk, when he comes upon a preacher baptising people in the river. He proceeds to walk into the water and subsequently bumps into the preacher. The preacher turns around and is almost overcome by the smell of alcohol, whereupon he asks the drunk, 'Are you ready to find Jesus?'

The drunk shouts, 'Yes, Oi am! So the preacher grabs him and dunks him in the water. He pulls him up and asks the drunk, 'Brother, have you found Jesus?' The drunk replies, 'No, Oi haven't found Jesus.'

The preacher, shocked at the answer, dunks him into the water again for a little longer. He again pulls him out of the water and asks again, 'Have you found Jesus me brother?' The drunk again answers, 'No, Oi I haven't found Jesus.'

By this time the preacher is at his wits end and dunks the drunk in the water again but this time holds him down for about 30 seconds and when he begins kicking his arms and legs he pulls him up.

He again asks the drunk. 'For the love of God, have you found Jesus yet?'

The drunk wipes his eyes, catches his breath and says to the preacher, 'Are you sure this is where he fell in?'

*Contributed by Vipin Buckshey, Delhi*

112

# THE SPICE OF LIFE

A beggar or a king
    In order to make life worth living
Man needs something spicy, something exciting.
    So when breaking furniture, howling and growling
Lose novelty
    People's representatives in the assembly
Strive hard to serve the country,
    For which they surf their iPads
To unearth crime, to root out obscenity
    And only by the way enjoy pornography
The affairs of the state
    The dull legislative business can wait
Because at the moment the scene is quite intimate
    Novelty today is custom tomorrow
So it is amusing to speculate
    How they will pass time in the assembly
Will they for the sake of novelty
    Actually enact something
That they most intently see?

*Contributed by Kuldip Salil, Delhi*


# POINTS OF VIEW

Virginity in females is a sign of purity; in males, it is a lack of opportunity!

*Contributed by Amarinder Bajaj, Delhi*

## WITCH HUNT

**F**uneral services were being conducted for a woman who had been thoroughly disliked in her rural community. With a violent, explosive disposition she hen-pecked her husband, drove her children mercilessly and quarrelled with her neighbours.

The day of the funeral was sultry, and as soon as the body was completely burnt a violent storm broke. There was a blinding flash of lightning, followed by a terrific clap of thunder. 'Well,' remarked one of the villagers, 'she's got there.'

*Contributed by Reeten Ganguly, Tezpur*

## REAL TEST

**D**ad: Hereafter don't call me Dad...

Kid: Oh, come on Dad, it was just a school test not the DNA test...!

*Contributed by Vipin Buckshey, Delhi*

## NO HAPPY RETURNS

A young girl invited a young man to her birthday.

Man: Congrats! I will come. Which birthday is it by the way?

Girl: Seventeenth.

Man: If I don't forget, last time also you said it was seventeenth.

Girl: Yes, I am not one of those who change their statements every other day. I stick to my word.

*Contributed by J C Mehta, Delhi*

## THINGS DIFFICULT TO ACHIEVE

To plant your idea in someone's head.
    To plant someone's money in your own pocket.
He who succeeds in the former, we call teacher.
    He who succeeds with the latter, we call boss.
The one who succeeds in both, we call wife.
    The one who fails in both, we call husband.

*Contributed by Vipin Buckshey, Delhi*

**S**on in India: A teenager who, without asking, will carry your grocery bags from the market.

Outside India: A teenager, who suddenly remembers he has homework when you start mowing the lawn.

~

Daughter in India: A lovely doll, who brings tears to your eyes during her marriage.

Outside India: A lovely doll, who brings you to tears long before her marriage.

~

Father in India: A person you are afraid of and who is never to be disobeyed.

Outside India: A person whom you pretend to obey, after all he is the one paying your college tuition.

~

Doctor in India: A respectable person with decent income.

Outside India: A money making machine, who has a money spending machine at home called 'doctor's wife.'

~

Bhangra in India: A vigorous Punjabi festival dance.

Outside India: A dance you do when you don't know how to dance.

*Contributed by Vipin Buckshey, New Delhi*

# MAN OR MOUSE

One night Santa came home drunk, so his wife beat him up. The next morning Banta saw his condition and learnt what had happened. 'You got beaten up by your wife? Are you a man or a mouse?' asked Banta tauntingly.

Santa: 'I am a man and I can prove it.'

Banta: 'How?'

Santa: My wife is afraid of mice.

A few days later, Banta came home drunk. He too was beaten up by his wife. The following morning Santa saw him and said, 'Oye, You got beaten up by your wife? Are you a man or a mouse? Squeak up!'

*Contributed by Vipin Buckshey, New Delhi*

# SILENCE ZONE

A friend who lives in a flat was listening to his music system on full volume one evening, when there was a knock at the door. It was his next door neighbour.

'Can you hear my TV?' asked the neighbour.

'No,' said my friend.

'Well,' said the neighbour, 'neither can I.'

*Contributed by Reeten Ganguly, Tezpur*

# TO PAKISTAN WITH LOVE

We love Pakistan for her Foreign Minister,
   if for nothing else
And the lovely smile on a lovely face that she could bring,
   Her manner sincere, her straight talk, her movements
      smooth.

And in spite of Pakistani media's gibberish uncouth,
   She is hopefully the face
and voice of Pakistan's maturity and youth.

The fanatics who would object to her Birkin bag
   And in entire womankind find a snag,
The same fanatics in colour whatever, anywhere
   Should be declared as diggers of grave.
Not only of peace and prosperity
   But of their community, religion and country.

Forgive them, O Lord, for they know not what they say,
   Perhaps their upbringing teaches them to bite and
      bray!

*Contributed by Kuldip Salil, Delhi*

# QUIRKY ENGLISH

Santa is taking grammar lessons:

'If more than one mouse is mice, then more than one spouse
is spice!!!!'

*Contributed by Meghna Lal, Noida*

## MONEY BACK

**A** salesman of a department store once told me that customers in the store where he works often complained about the rising cost of greeting cards. He never took their comments seriously until the day a woman asked him, 'Do you have any birthday cards for someone turning 100?' He led her to the appropriate rack, where she picked up a card and checked the price. 'If she doesn't make it,' asked the customer, 'can I bring it back?'

*Contributed by Reeten Ganguly, Tezpur*


## MERI DILLI, MERI SHAAN

*Yahan khuda hai, wahan khuda hai...*
*idhar khuda hai, udhar khuda hai...*
*jahan nahin khuda hain, wahan kal khudega...*

*Contributed by Neha Sharma, New Delhi*

## NEAT ANALYSIS

The doctor diagnosed the Anglo-Indian colonel's illness as hydropsy, 'What is that?' the colonel asked.

'To much water in the body,' the doctor explained.

The whisky-drinking colonel was indignant: 'But I have never drunk a drop of water all my life, doctor.'

He then paused and sadly concluded: 'Must have been the ice.'

*Contributed by Reeten Ganguly, Tezpur*

## PARADISE REGAINED, PARADISE LOST

A patient in a hospital saw a beautiful nurse and exclaimed, 'I feel I am in Heaven!'

His wife standing next to him said, 'No darling, I am still with you.'

*Contributed by Brij Mehra, New Delhi*

## OXYMORON

Some examples of oxymorons used about Americans when they couldn't find weapons of mass destruction in Iraq: American intelligence, mother of all, happily married.

*Contributed by Vipin Buckshey, New Delhi*

## THE REASON WHY

**R**ahul complained to his mother: 'Mama, I can't marry anyone because of you.'

Sonia: 'Why *beta*? What have I done?'

Rahul: 'Wherever I go people shout: *"Sonia ko bahumat do."*'

*Contributed by Vipin Buckshey, New Delhi*

## FIRST PRIORITY

Rohan: 'Why are you looking so annoyed?'

Sohan: 'Because that pretty girl called me Uncle.'

Rohan: 'So, what is wrong with that?'

Sohan: 'Well, she is around 25 years old, and I am just 35. How can she call me Uncle?'

Rohan: 'It is just a pity you are not from the South, like me. I would not mind her calling me Uncle at all.'

Sohan: 'Why?'

Rohan: 'Because in the part of the country I come from, a maternal uncle has first priority for marrying a girl.'

*Contributed by Reeten Ganguly, Tezpur*


## PARLIAMENTARY ACHIEVEMENT

Ever wondered why so little gets done in Indian Parliament?

Rudyard Kipling, the novelist of the British Raj, explained it clearly long ago, 'Every one wanted to say so much that no one said anything in particular.'

*Manas Chakravarty in Hindustan Times*

## SANTA'S FERRARI

 **S**anta shows up at his friend Banta's place in a brand new red Ferarri.

Banta: 'Wow Santa, *ki gaddi hai!* (What a car!) *Kithon laiye* (where did you get it from)?'

Santa: '*Main highway te lift mang reya si... gori mem aaee te mainu kendi,* "Want a ride Mr. Singh?"

I hopped in, and she took me to the woods. Once in woods she got out of the car, took off her clothes and said to me, "Mr Singh take anything".'

Banta is quite excited and asks, '*Te tu ki keeta, Santa?* (So, what did you do?)'

Santa: '*Main gaddi lai layee.* (I took the car.)'

Banta: '*Changa keeta, kapde tenu fit bhi nahi aane si.* (Good show, you wouldn't have fit into her clothes).'

*Contributed by Saksham Jain, New Delhi*

## MODERN ART

**J**asbir visits an art gallery: 'I suppose this horrible looking thing is what you call modern art?'

Art dealer: 'I beg your pardon sir, that is a mirror.'

*Contributed by Sanjay Shah, Mumbai*

President Obama was sitting in his oval office in USA wondering whom to invade next when his telephone rang. 'Hello, Mr Obama!' A heavily accented voice said, 'This is Gurmukh from Phagwara, District Kapurthala, Punjab. I am ringing to inform you that we are officially declaring the war on you!'

'Well, Gurmukh,' Obama replied, 'This is indeed important news! How big is your army?'

'Right now,' said Gurmukh, after a moment's calculation, there is myself, my cousin Sukhdev, my next door neighbour Bhagat, and the entire kabaddi team from the Gurudwara. That makes eight!'

Obama paused, 'I must tell you, Gurmukh that I have one million men in my army waiting to move on my command.'

'*Ohh, ho! Main kya ji...*' said Gurmukh, 'I'll have to ring you back!'

Sure enough, the next day, Gurmukh called again. 'Mr Obama, it is Gurmukh, I'm calling from Phagwara STD booth, the war is still on! We have managed to acquire some infantry equipment!'

'And what equipment would that be, Gurmukh', Obama asked. 'Well, we have two combines, a donkey and Amrik's tractor.' Obama sighed. 'I must tell you, Gurmukh, that I have 16,000 tanks and 14,000 armoured personnel carriers. I also have increased my army to 1.5 million since we last spoke.'

'*Oh teri...*' said Gurmukh. 'I'll have to get back to you.'

Sure enough, Gurmukh rang again the next day. 'Mr Obama, the war is still on! We have managed to get ourselves airborne. We've modified Amrik's tractor by adding a couple of shotguns, sticking on some wings and the *pind's* generator. Four school-pass boys from Malpur have joined us as well!'

Obama was silent for a minute and then cleared his throat. 'I must tell you, Gurmukh, that I have 10,000 bombers and 20,000 fighter planes. My military complex is surrounded by laser-guided surface-to-air-missile sites. And since we last spoke, I've increased my army to two million!'

'*Tera bhala hove, oye...*' said Gurmukh, 'I'll have to ring you back.'

Sure enough, Gurmukh called again the next day. '*Kiddan,* Mr Obama? (How are you, Mr. Obama?) I am sorry to tell you that we have had to call off the war.'

'I am sorry to hear that,' said Obama. 'Why the sudden change of heart?'

'Well,' said Gurmukh, 'we've all had a long chat over a couple of *lassis* and decided there is no way we can feed two million prisoners of wars!'

Now that is called the Punjabi confidence.

*Contributed by Paramjit S Kochar, Delhi*

## MISSING AND LOST

 **H**aving lost his donkey Santa got down to his knees and started thanking God.

Banta, his friend, asks, 'Your donkey is missing and you are thanking God; what for?'

Santa replies, 'I am thanking Him for seeing to it that I wasn't riding the donkey at that time, otherwise I, too, would have been missing.'

*Contributed by Brijesh Kapoor, Ludhiana*


## UNLETTRED BUT EDUCATED

**S**anta: *'Kinna padhey likhe ho?'* (How much are you educated?)

Banta: 'B.A.'

Santa: *'Bewakoof do akshar padha, woh bhi ulta!'* (Idiot! Knows only two letters and those also in wrong order.)

*Contributed by Vinay Thakur, Jalpaiguri*

## RSVP

 **S**anta and Jeeto were at the printers preparing invitation cards for their son's wedding.

Jeeto was not very good at English so she asked the printer to help her. After the printer had presented her with a draft, she quickly pointed out that the 'RSVP' was missing.

The printer was surprised by Jeeto's knowledge and asked her if she knew what it meant.

After much thought Jeeto replied, 'Wait! I remember. RSVP. It means Remember, Send Vedding Present.'

*Contributed by Gaurav Samarth, Faridabad*

## GREETINGS

**A**n Englishman and Santa met inside a toilet.

Englishman: 'Good evening, how do your do?'

Santa: 'Good evening, we open the zip and do!'

*Contributed by Anusha Bindal, New Delhi*

# BECADSE YOU ARE MY SON...

**S**anta returns from his first day at school and immediately questions his father, 'Papa, today we had a spelling class. All the other kids could only say half the alphabet, but I knew the whole thing. Is that because I am your son?'

'No son, that's because you are intelligent.'

Santa seemed content with the answer, asks his father another question, 'Papa, today we had Maths class. All the other kids could only count from 1 to 10, I could count from 1 to 20. Is this because I am your son?'

'No son, that's because you are intelligent,' replies his father.

Happy with the answer, Santa poses another question to his father, 'Papa, today we had medical examination, all the other boys were shorter than me, I was at least twice their height. Is that because I am your son?'

The father replies, 'No son, that's because you are 33 years old.'

*Contributed by Kusumlata, Imphal*

## ARAB IN YANKEE LAND

 **M**ohammad, a child of Arab parents was enrolled in a school in New York.

On the first day, his teacher asked, 'What is your name?' The boy replied, 'Mohammad'.

'From now on your name is Harry as you are in America,' she said.

In the evening, when he came back, his mother asked, 'How was your day Mohammad?' He said, 'My name is not Mohammad. I'm in America and my name is Harry.'

His mother slapped him and said angrily: 'Aren't you ashamed of trying to dishonour your parents, your heritage, your religion?' Then she called his father and he also slapped him.

The next day when the teacher saw him with his face red and asked what happened, Mohammad said, 'Madam, four hours after I became American, I was attacked by two Arabs.'

*Contributed by JP Singh Kaka, Bhopal*

## TELL ME THE MEANING...

**S**anta: *'Yar iska matlab kya hota hai,* "I AM GOING"?'

Banta: *'Main jaa raha hun.'*

Santa: *'Ruk, aise kaise jayega, 20 aur bhi aise hi ja chuke hain... answer bata ke jaa.'*

*Contributed by Sudha Paladugu, Hyderabad*

## HEAVENLY FARE

**A** man goes to heaven after doing good work on earth. He could see hell from his place in heaven. To his surprise, he saw a sumptuous feast was on. If people in hell could get such delightful food, he wondered what was awaiting him. But a bearer left just a *sukhi roti* and a stale pickle as his meal. 'I say, I am in heaven and you are serving such poor food when hellish people are enjoying a feast,' he remarked in anger.

'I know, I know, but which contractor would prepare food just for you alone? So you get whatever is available.'

*Contributed by G Neelakantan, Bangalore*

## LOVE SET

**T**he two warring superstars of Indian tennis finally made up. To celebrate, they went to a five-star hotel for dinner. After the meal was over, the waiter presented the bill to Mahesh Bhupathi. Mahesh gestured towards his companion and said, 'Leander Paes.'

*Contributed by Rajeshwari Singh, Delhi*

# THE ART OF DENIAL

Kapil Sibal, a central minister, penned this poem. Some excerpts:

Ajmal Kasab trained to be a terrorist, Pakistani.
But Pakis say they do not know
We'll have to prove if that is so.
His parents at Faridkot claim
This is our child the one they named.
Since then they have been whisked away
Where they are now? No one can say.
Be upfront says Nawaz Sharif
Your version is beyond belief
Denial of open access,
Why bar parents to meet the press?
House out of bounds most Indians feel
You'd rather have the truth concealed.
Your plea, government unfairly blamed...
...Non-State actors even if Pak
Their whereabouts cannot be tracked
Arrest, wanted Azhar Masood
Will vitiate our national mood
Arresting him would not be right
We have no means to extradite
The fallback is we are in doubt
Do not quite know his whereabouts
We did admit erroneously
That he is in our custody
If you question our honesty
Will deny his identity.

*Contributed by J P Singh Kaka, Bhopal*

## HELP-BOOK(S)

An old lady who was suffering from severe constipation went to her doctor. 'My bowels haven't moved for seven days. I am in agony.'

'Have you done anything about it?' asked the doctor.

'I sit on the commode every morning and evening.'

'Do you take anything?'

'Of course, I take a book.'

*Contributed by Amarinder Bajaj, Delhi*


## SAFE HAVEN(S)

No one is safe in Pakistan
  Not even 'Osama Bin Laden'
Everyone is safe in Hindustan
  Even 'Ajmal Kasab'...

*Contributed by Vipin Buckshey, New Delhi*

Unless you can look interested when you are bored, you will never be a success socially.

🎭

Early to bed and early to rise is a sure sign that you don't care for television.

🎭

You can't fall out of bed if you sleep on the floor.

🎭

One advantage of being stupid is that you never get lonely.

🎭

The first half of our lives is ruined by our parents and second half by our children.

🎭

Speech is a faculty given to man to conceal his thoughts.

🎭

Men have sight, women insight.

🎭

I quote others to better express myself.

🎭

A snorer is a sound sleeper.

🎭

A reformer is one who makes others feel miserable about their pleasures.

When prices are high, money does not talk, it whispers.

☙

If you can't think of any other way to flatter a man, tell him he is the one that can't be flattered.

☙

The hardest trial of heart is whether it can bear a rival's failure without triumph.

☙

There is no arena in which vanity displays itself under such a variety of forms as in conversation.

*Contributed by Rajnish Sharma, Shimla*


## FAIR DEMAND

Robber: 'Give me all your money!'

Hold up victim: 'Don't you know who I am? I am a Member of Parliament.'

Robber: 'Ok. Give me all *my* money.'

*Contributed by Tanmay Kathuria, Noida*

## BLESSED HUSBANDS

Husbands are an unpredictable lot
    Ever craving for what can't be got
When things are cold, they like it hot
    Always wanting what is not.
God help them!

Then heart's desire, now they have won with their pretty
      spouse,
    poised ever ready to come
Life becomes one long, long stretch of fun
    With all play and not an ounce of work done.
God bless them!

*Contributed by Rajmani Kumar, Jharkhand*


## LOVE AS TARGET

Rohan's wife had gone to her mother's place. While she was away, Rohan was using her enlarged photo as a dart board. His aim, however, was lousy and his darts rarely hit their target. One day, his wife rang him up.

Wife: 'How are you pulling on in my absence?'

Rohan: 'I can truly and truthfully say that I am missing you a lot.'

*Contributed by Rajeshwari Singh, New Delhi*

## BRIGHT IDEAS

What do you call a male ladybird?

When they say dog food is new and improved in taste, who tastes it?

If the 'black box' flight recorder is never damaged during a plane crash, why isn't the whole airplane made out of that stuff?

Can you cry under water?

Why doesn't glue stick to its bottle?

Why do you still call it a building when it is already built?

If you aren't supposed to drink and drive, why do bars have parking lots?

*Contributed by Vipin Buckshey, New Delhi*

## HAPPY MARRIAGE

**S**anta took his wife who was in poor health to the doctor. The doctor examined her thoroughly. 'It's bad news,' he told Santa. 'She has got cancer and will not last for more than six months.'

Santa took the doctor's verdict with a smile. 'Somehow when I have spent 25 years plus with her, I can spend another six months also.'

*Contributed by Bubble Charanjit Singh, Delhi*


## INDIA AT CROSSROADS

**T**he writer, actor and director Woody Allen warned us long ago of the tough choices we faced in electing our leaders. Should we choose the Congress or the BJP? Should we go right or left?

This is what he said: 'More than any other time in history, mankind faces a crossroads. One path leads to despair and utter hopelessness. The other, to total extinction. Let us pray we have the wisdom to choose correctly.'

*Contributed by Karan Thapar, New Delhi*

## TART FOR PLEASURE

At the Delhi Golf Club, the last week of each year is abuzz with fervour and gaiety with members merrily exchanging season's greetings. On one such day, my host and I arrived late for lunch and found that all the dessert was over. With dogged determination and the perseverance of a man with a sweet tooth, I was able to grab a solitary portion of lemon tart. With only one piece to share, the following conversation transpired:

'May I split the lemon tart in two halves, so that both of us can have half a portion each?'

Host: 'No, instead you take the full portion of lemon and relish it, leaving the tart for my exclusive pleasure.'

*Contributed by Colonel Trilok Mehrotra, New Delhi*


## GENDER-BENDER

Teacher: 'What is the difference between a man and a woman?'

Student: 'Man has a great sense of humour whereas a woman has a great sense of rumour.'

*Contributed by Vipin Buckshey, Delhi*

## STICK AND GUN

Gill who tamed terrorism in Punjab
    Failed in the sports field
Why? Don't take it as fun
    Hockey is a stick, not a gun!

*Contributed by GC Bhandari, Meerut*

**W**ho said Indians don't have a sense of wit? We can be as inventive and clever as any one else in the world, are bloody good devising puns and rhymes. In fact our command of multiple languages and cultures makes the possibilities seemingly endless.

First, there are straight puns. Or simple homonyms, i.e. two words that sound the same but have different meanings. However, in each case they're also placed in apparent opposition to each other.

The simple ones are:

'Missionary by day, missionary by night';
'Pray by day and prey by night' and
'Dear God by day, Thank God by night'.

One step better are those that combine different cultures and languages to achieve the same effect. Here are a few:

'Ram by day, ram by night';
'Holy by day, holi *hai* by night' and
'Swami by day, show me by night'.

Next are the aphorisms that rely on a very apposite sense of rhyme. Once again, notice the cross-cultural and multi-lingual use of words:

'Sandalwood by day, Tiger Woods by night';
'Monk by day, Old Monk by night';
'Monk by day, bonk by night';
'Renounce by day, pounce by night';
'*Chamatkar* by day, *balatkar* by night';

'Sri Sri by day, *Stri Stri* by night';
'Shiva disciple by day, Chivas disciple by night';
'*Swahaa* by day, Aaah aaaaaha by night';
'Moral by day, oral by night';
'God-man by day, lay-man by night';
'Discourse by day, intercourse by night';
'Seer by day, leer by night';
'Mahadev by day, Kamdev by night';
'Shivlinga by day, cunnilingus by night'.

However, my favourites are neither pun nor rhyme but rely on an inspired twist in meaning. Some are astonishingly clever. Here are a few:

'Spiritual by day, spirited by night';
'Saffron by day, blue by night';
'Do-gooder by day, Good-doer by night';
'Incense by day, incest by night';
'Divine message by day, divine massage by night'.

*Contributed by Karan Thapar, New Delhi*

## LOVING NURSE

**S**anta falls in love with a nurse. After much thinking, he finally writes a love letter to her: 'I luv u, sister.'

*Contributed by Brij Mehra, New Delhi*

## MULTI-RACIAL

On a train from London to Manchester, an American was berating the Englishman sitting across from him in the compartment. 'You English are too stuffy. You set yourselves apart too much. You think your stiff upper lip makes you above the rest of us. Look at me. I have Italian blood, French blood, a little Indian blood, and some Swedish blood. What do you say to that?'

The Englishman replied: 'Awfully sporting of your mother, old chap.'

*Contributed by Vipin Buckshey, Delhi*

## SUPER-FAST

Banta: 'Name the three fastest means of communication.'
Santa: 'Telephone, television, tell-a-woman.'

*Contributed by Brij Mehra, New Delhi*

## REDEFINED!

What is old age?

When you start turning off the lights for economical reasons instead of romantic ones.

*Contributed by Gurpreet Singh, Ludhiana*